DUMBASS TOO
The Collected Quotes of Donald J Trump:
The Most Dangerous Mouth in the World

All Rights Reserved ©

Ampersand Ink
Horton Press
581 Armour Road
Peterborough, On
Canada

Printed in the United States of America

To Brian,
For doing all the dishes.

Acknowledgements

Adam, my steady source of reason in an unreasonable world.

Brian, for the love, the laughs and the gas.

Gabe, Isa, Sojo and Peter…my noisiest, messiest, cuddliest sources of happiness.

My Family — My favourite party animals.

Table of Contents

Introduction
7

Foreword: Dear America
9

Trump on Trump
13

Family Man
63

Pervert-in-Chief
81

Birther-in-Chief
139

Racist-in-Chief
171

Commander-in-Chief
215

Contradictor-in-Chief
275

Campaigner-in-Chief
325

Tweeter-in-Chief
367

Introduction

The original DUMBASS was published in 2006, at the height of Dick Cheney's reign...err...I mean, George W. Bush's second term. I was angry back then...well, insulted mostly...because the President of the United States was barely able to string together two coherent words. To me, the election of George W Bush was the death knell of the American democratic system....a symbol of everything that is broken or corrupted by a system run amok.

But, DUMBASS was funny. Bushisms can be hilarious. It was a fun book, despite what I felt it represented.

But, DUMBASS TOO is not delivering much in the yucks department. Donald Trump's words are angry, often lies and without his two-bit Bronx accent, his quotes are not as much fun as Bush's. Trump doesn't trip over his words very often, only his ego. Even my quips, lean more towards the sarcastic than the funny....and so I only made them when I just couldn't help myself. Mostly, my comments are to give context when needed.

The book is not an exhaustive text — because Donald Trump has been around for a long, long time and he never, ever shuts up.

No, DUMBASS TOO is just a highlight reel. I'm sure there will be more to come in the next few years — at least until someone says something mean to Donald on Twitter and he launches the nuclear warheads.

Foreword

December 3, 2016

Dear America,

I'm not delusional. I know that the person who voted Trump is not the same person who will read this book. You know what just happened (election night 2016), and so do I.

You don't need me to explain to you all the reasons why Donald Trump is a danger to himself and others. We get swept up in the exact same wave of nausea every time he flaps his racist, ignorant pie-hole.

But, unfortunately, Donald Trump isn't just any bloomin' idiot…He's an outside bloomin' idiot.

And when he touts himself as an "outsider," it only serves to remind us that this guy, not only doesn't know the first thing about running a country, it reminds us that he isn't remotely interested in learning how.

His first campaign manager said that Donald isn't one to "roll up his sleeves," he sees himself more as a Chairman of the Board than a CEO or, God forbid, a COO. Donald doesn't like to work; so they will need to find people to do the work for him. You didn't elect those people…and you didn't elect a Royal Family to take over the White House.

Ivanka is not the First Lady, although I like her more than Melania, but the notion that she will take up Melania's duties and represent the country and potentially take up a pet policy position infuriates me. Not that I don't think she'll be good at it, but the nepotism stinks to high heaven, and now her husband, who was responsible for a great deal of strife on the transition team, and who could not be given a key role in the administration, will likely have Donald's ear on a daily basis anyway. He is Rasputin to the Tsar.

Meanwhile, Melania will stay in New York, like a spoiled brat, and her security detail will cost the city over $1 million per day. Who can run up a security bill of nearly half a billion dollars per year without batting an eye? The truly vain and entitled, that's who.

Voters got caught up in the idea that if Donald ran the country like he runs his businesses, everything would be fixed. But, Donald isn't a great business man; He's not even a good one. He is responsible for, or tied to, an enormous string of failures, such as:

Trump University, Trump Steaks, Trump Vodka, Trump Ice, Trump Air, Trump Institute, Trump Mortgage, Trump Taj Mahal, Trump Castle, Trump Tower Tampa, the New Jersey Generals and the United States Football League, Trump Magazine, Trump World Magazine, Trump the game, Trump New Media, GoTrump.com, Trump Network (MLM vitamin sales), Tour de Trump, Trump on the Ocean, Trumped the radio show, Trumpnet (Internet service provider) – and then there is Trump Tower Chicago, Trump Boca and numerous other failed real estate projects around the globe that have cost buyers and investors hundreds of millions of dollars.

No, if Donald runs his country like he ran his businesses, he will swoop in with a bunch of lies and big talk, then he will fuck it into the ground while redecorating national landmarks with tacky gold paint...Trump's taste is "80's ostentatious." He will break every rule to line his own pockets and once there is nothing left to loot, he will take your watch and wallet and scurry off into the night shouting, "BANKRUPTCY!!," like the thieving little rat he is.

To Donald, this election was about winning; not about governing. He didn't look ahead to what happens after he achieved his singular goal. Now, a temperamental bully has been armed and left in charge.

Trump doesn't have the intellect, maturity, discretion or broad, steady shoulders needed to run a country...He knows nothing about the actual job and has appointed rich cronies to key cabinet positions who also know nothing about their jobs. It's either a sitcom or a nightmare.

Our only real hope is that he gets bored or overwhelmed and bows out. I am certain that if he lasts this first four years that he will not win a second election – I doubt he will even try. But, he can still try to shred the Constitution while he's there. He can still do some damage.

Now it is time to protect yourselves against the interloper. Unite and fight to protect what you hold dear. Challenge everything. Peaceful protests. Call your state representatives every day, if necessary.

They are the key to stopping Donald in his tracks. Every single one of them is elected by their constituents and likely wants to keep their job. Remind them whom they work for. Then remind them again and again and again. I don't see any other way.

I'm rooting for you.

Jules

TRUMP
ON TRUMP

"I do whine because I want to win, and I'm not happy about not winning, and I am a whiner, and I keep whining and whining until I win."

"The show is "Trump" and it is sold-out performances everywhere. I've had fun doing it and will continue to have fun, and I think most people enjoy it."
Playboy, March 1990

"I like it when people talk about me. As long as it is positive."
(LifeBeyondSport.com, undated)

"What do people say about me? Do they say I'm loyal? Do they say I work hard?"
Village Voice, Jan. 15, 1979

"I really value my reputation and I don't hesitate to sue."
Village Voice, Jan. 15, 1979

"Man is the most vicious of all animals, and life is a series of battles ending in victory or defeat."
People Interview, 1981

"I don't like to lose."
New York Times, Aug. 7, 1983

"The mind can overcome any obstacle. I never think of the negative."
New York Times, Aug. 7, 1983

Glad I added a chapter on contradictions later.

"I know how to sell. Selling is life. You can have the greatest singer in the world, but if nobody knows who he is, he'll never have the opportunity to sing."
Sports Illustrated, Feb. 13, 1984

"When I build something for somebody, I always add $50 million or $60 million onto the price. My guys come in, they say it's going to cost $75 million. I say it's going to cost $125 million, and I build it for $100 million. Basically, I did a lousy job. But they think I did a great job."
Team Owners Meeting USFL, 1984

Bragging about how he profits from doing lousy work....his words, not mine.

"When I think I'm right, nothing bothers me."
60 Minutes, September 3, 1985

"I don't even consider myself ambitious."
60 Minutes", 1985

"I believe [the media] like making me out to be something more sinister than I really am."
60 Minutes, 1985

"Let me tell you something about the rich. They have a very low threshold for pain."
New York magazine, February 11, 1985

"Controversy, in short, sells."
The Art of the Deal, 1987

"There are people — I categorize them as life's losers — who get their sense of accomplishment and achievement from trying to stop others. As far as I'm concerned, if they had any real ability, they wouldn't be fighting me, they'd be doing something constructive themselves."
The Art of the Deal, 1987

I decided to do both.

"In the second grade I actually gave a teacher a black eye — I punched my music teacher because I didn't think he knew anything about music and I almost got expelled."
The Art of the Deal, 1987

….and so it began.

"I don't do it for the money. I do it to do it."
The Art of the Deal, 1987

Those lines were actually written by Tony Schwartz in The Art of the Deal....because Trump really does do it for the money.

"People think I'm a gambler. I've never gambled in my life. To me, a gambler is someone who plays slot machines. I prefer to own slot machines. It's a very good business being the house."
The Art of the Deal, 1987

"I like the casino business. I like the scale, which is huge, I like the glamour, and most of all, I like the cash flow."
The Art of the Deal, 1987

Until you declare bankruptcy four times.

"And while I can't honestly say I need an 80-foot living room, I do get a kick out of having one."
The Art of the Deal, 1987

"Yes. He was still an odd person then… to me, Donald Trump is not a rich man. Donald Trump is like what a hobo imagines a rich man to be. Like Trump was walking around under an underpass, and he heard some guy like 'Ohh, as soon as my number comes in, I'm gonna put up tall buildings with my name on 'em! I'll have fine golden hair, and a TV show where I fire Gene Simmons with my children.' And Trump was like 'That is how I will live my life.'"

– **John Mulaney**

"I aim very high, and then I just keep pushing and pushing and pushing to get what I'm after."
The Art of the Deal, 1987

"I'll do nearly anything within legal bounds to win."
The Art of the Deal, 1987

"The way I see it, critics get to say what they want about my work, so why shouldn't I be able to say what I want to about theirs?"
The Art of the Deal, 1987

> During one down period, I referred to him in print as a "financially embattled thousandaire" and he sent me a copy of the column with my picture circled and "The Face of a Dog!" written over it.
> **— Gail Collins, New York Times**

"Sometimes, part of making a deal is denigrating your competition."
The Art of the Deal, 1987

"It's been said that I believe in the power of positive thinking. In fact, I believe in the power of negative thinking."
The Art of the Deal, 1987

"I play to people's fantasies. People may not always think big themselves, but they can still get very excited by those who do. That's why a little hyperbole never hurts."
The Art of the Deal, 1987

"People want to believe that something is the biggest and the greatest and the most spectacular."
The Art of the Deal, 1987

"Most people think small, because most people are afraid of success, afraid of making decisions, afraid of winning. And that gives people like me a great advantage."
The Art of the Deal, 1987

"The point is, you can never be too greedy."
The Art of the Deal, 1987

"One thing I've learned about the press is that they're always hungry for a good story, and the more sensational the better. ... The point is that if you are a little different, or a little outrageous, or if you do things that are bold or controversial, the press is going to write about you."
The Art of the Deal, 1987

"Sometimes they write positively, and sometimes they write negatively. But from a pure business point of view, the benefits of being written about have far outweighed the drawbacks."
The Art of the Deal, 1987

"Sometimes it pays to be a little wild."
The Art of the Deal, 1987

"I've always felt that a lot of modern art is a con, and that the most successful painters are often better salesmen and promoters than they are artists."
The Art of the Deal, 1987

Same can be said about politicians

"I'm not big on compromise. I understand compromise. Sometimes compromise is the right answer, but oftentimes compromise is the equivalent of defeat, and I don't like being defeated."
Life Magazine, January 1989

"I've always been thin-skinned. I've been thin-skinned from day one."
CNN, March 29, 1990

Rare moment of personal insight…savour it. There won't be any more.

"I enjoy testing friendship…. Everything in life to me is a psychological game, a series of challenges you either meet or don't. I am always testing people who work for me."
Playboy Interview, 1990

"I will send people around to my buyers to test their honesty by offering them trips and other things. I've been surprised that some people least likely to accept a trip from a contractor did and some of the most likely did not. You can never tell until you test; the human species is interesting in that way. So to me, friendship can be really tested only in bad times."
Playboy 1990

What a lonely world he must live in…

"I instinctively mistrust many people. It is not a negative in my life but a positive. Playboy wouldn't be talking to me today if I weren't a cynic."
Playboy 1990

"The real public feels that Donald Trump is going through Trump-bashing. When I go out now, forget about it. I'm mobbed. It's bedlam."
Vanity Fair, September 1990

"I made a lot of money and I made it too easily, to the point of boredom."
Vanity Fair, September 1990

It's like taking candy from a golden baby…

"the same assets that excite me in the chase, often, once they are acquired, leave me bored. For me, you see, the important thing is the getting, not the having."
Surviving at the Top, 1990

"There has always been a display of wealth and always will be, until the depression comes, which it always does. And let me tell you, a display is a good thing. It shows people that you can be successful. It can show you a way of life. "Dynasty" did it on TV. It's very important that people aspire to be successful. The only way you can do it is if you look at somebody who is."
Playboy, March 1990

I hate to think of Dynasty being a cultural benchmark.

Playboy: How large a role does pure ego play in your deal making and enjoyment of publicity?

Trump: Every successful person has a very large ego."
Playboy: Every successful person? Mother Teresa? Jesus Christ?

Trump: Far greater egos than you will ever understand.
Playboy, March 1990

"I do think Donald Trump is honest in his own way. He is honestly an egomaniacal billionaire."
–Stephen Colbert

"Nothing wrong with ego."
Playboy, March 1990

> "Give them the old Trump bullshit," he told the architect Der Scutt before a presentation of the Trump Tower design at a press conference in 1980. "Tell them it is going to be a million square feet, sixty-eight stories." "I don't lie, Donald," the architect replied
> **Vanity Fair Sept 1990**

"I've had a lot of victories. I fight hard for victory, and I think I enjoy it as much as I ever did. But I realize that maybe new victories won't be the same as the first couple."
People, July 9, 1990

"I truly believe that someone successful is never really happy, because dissatisfaction is what drives him."
Playboy, March 1990

"I don't sleep more than four hours a night."
Playboy, March 1990

More time for Twitter!

"I'm never self-satisfied."
Playboy, March 1990

"How long is your article?"
Vanity Fair, September 1990

He measures his penis in column inches...

"Is it a cover?"
Vanity Fair, September 1990

"My attention span is short."
Trump: Surviving at the Top, 1990

"I know what sells and I know what people want."
Playboy, March 1990

"Publicity gradually dehumanizes you."
Trump: Surviving at the Top, 1990

"People are too trusting. I'm a very untrusting guy."
Playboy, March 1990

"It's fame itself that bends people out of shape. In fact, the more celebrities I meet, the more I realize that fame is a kind of drug, one that is way too powerful for most people to handle."
Trump: Surviving at the Top, 1990

"I do believe in hate when it's appropriate."
Trump: Surviving at the Top, 1990

"L.A. is going to be very hot, and it is very hot. The fact that Trump goes there makes it even hotter."
New York Times, February 5, 1990

"Anyone who thinks he's going to win them all is going to wind up a big loser."
> **Trump: Surviving at the Top, 1990**

"Toughness is knowing how to be a gracious winner—and rebounding quickly when you lose."
> **Trump: Surviving at the Top, 1990**

Wise words from a ghost writer

"I'm not the world's happiest person."
> **New York magazine, March 5, 1990**

> And they got on the elevator and Trump looked miserable. I was on the elevator alone with him, just by chance, and he just looked miserable. He looked so unhappy. All that money, I realized that he has all these billions of dollars, but he's fuckin' miserable because he needs $100 billion to look in the mirror and not want to kill himself. He needs that."
>
> — **Louis C.K.**

"Donald is a believer in the big-lie theory," his lawyer had told me. "If you say something again and again, people will believe you."

"One of my lawyers said that?" Trump said when I asked him about it. "I think if one of my lawyers said that, I'd like to know who it is, because I'd fire his ass. I'd like to find out who the scumbag is!"

Vanity Fair, September, 1990

"Did you see that The New York Times said I looked like Robert Redford?"
Vanity Fair, September, 1990

"I'm more popular now than I was two months ago. There are two publics as far as I'm concerned. The real public and then there's the New York society horseshit. The real public has always liked Donald Trump."
Vanity Fair, September, 1990

"I'm a bit of a P.T. Barnum; I make stars out of everyone."
The London Observer, 1991

> "He's an obscenely wealthy version of Erik Estrada or William Shatner, a cultural punch line who still has to exist as a human. And the worst part is that no matter how many times he tells us how mean he is, he needs us to like him so badly."
>
> **—Tom Scharpling**

"I'm a guy who lies awake at night and thinks and plots."
New York magazine, Nov. 9, 1992

"You may get AIDS by kissing."
The Howard Stern Show, 1993

"Hey, look, I had a cold spell from 1990 to '91. I was beat up in business and in my personal life. But you learn that you're either the toughest, meanest piece of shit in the world or you just crawl into a corner, put your finger in your mouth, and say, 'I want to go home.' You

never know until you're under pressure how you're gonna react. Guys that I thought were tough were nothin'."
New York magazine, Aug. 15, 1994

"Not bad. Beautiful wife, beautiful girlfriend, everything beautiful. Life was a bowl of cherries."
Primetime Live, 1994

"Look at these contracts. I get these to sign every day. I've signed hundreds of these. Here's a contract for $2.2 million. It's a building that isn't even opened yet. It's eighty-three percent sold, and nobody even knows it's there. For each contract, I need to sign twenty-two times, and if you think that's easy … You know, all the buyers want my signature. I had someone else who works for me signing, and at the closings the buyers got angry. I told myself, 'You know, these people are paying a million eight, a million seven, two million nine, four million one—for those kinds of numbers, I'll sign the fucking contract.' I understand. Fuck it. It's just more work."
New Yorker, May 19, 1997

"My attitude is if somebody's willing to pay me $225,000 to make a speech, it seems stupid not to show up. You know why I'll do it? Because I don't think anyone's ever been paid that much."
New Yorker, May 19, 1997

It was 3 speeches at $75k a pop...and lots of people got paid that much.

> "Donald Trump is the weak man's vision of a strong man."
> **—Charles Cooke**

"People say the '80s are dead, all the luxury, the extravagance. I say, 'What?' Am I supposed to change my taste because it's a new decade? That's bullshit."
Playboy, May 1997

Because pooping into a golden toilet never goes out of style.

"I always go into the center."
New Yorker, May 19, 1997

"The press portrays me as a wild flamethrower. In actuality, I think I'm much different from that. I think I'm totally inaccurately portrayed."
The New Yorker, May 19, 1997

"You gotta say, I cover the gamut. Does the kid cover the gamut? Boy, it never ends. I mean, people have no idea. Cool life. You know, it's sort of a cool life."
New Yorker, May 19, 1997

"You want to know what total recognition is? I'll tell you how you know you've got it. When the Nigerians on the street corners who don't speak a word of English, who have no clue, who're selling watches for some guy in New Jersey—when you walk by and those guys say, 'Trump! Trump!' That's total recognition."
New Yorker, May 19, 1997

"It's always good to do things nice and complicated so that nobody can figure it out."
New Yorker, May 19, 1997

"I put my name on buildings because it sells better. I don't do it because, gee, I need that."
Larry King Live, October 18, 1999

"I am very skeptical about people; that's self-preservation at work. I believe that, unfortunately, people are out for themselves. At this point, it's to many people's advantage to like me."
Larry King Live, October 8, 1999

"How do you define leadership? I mean, leadership is a very strange word because, you know, some people have it, some people don't and nobody knows why."
Larry King Live, 1999

Proof that he's never read a book that didn't have his name on it....likely proof that he's never read any of those either.

"I'm intelligent. Some people would say I'm very, very, very intelligent."
Fortune, April 3, 2000

"Because I've been successful, make money, get headlines, and have authored bestselling books, I have a better chance to make my ideas public than do people who are less well known."
The America We Deserve, 2000

"Money is a little bit of a scorecard, but I don't do it for the money. I do it because I really enjoy it. I love the creative process."
Late Edition with Wolf Blitzer, March 21, 2004

"When I go to restaurants, especially since The Apprentice, I always get free meals—"Oh please, Mr. Trump, there's no charge"—even if I'm there with 10 or 15 people. The sad part is, if I were someone who needed money I'd have to pay."
Playboy, October 2004

I appreciate the irony.

"I was very bad. That's why my parents sent me to a military academy. I was rebellious. Not violent or anything, but I wasn't exactly well behaved. I once gave one of my teachers a black eye. I talked back to my parents and to people in general. Perhaps it was more like bratty behaviour, but I certainly wasn't the perfect child.

Playboy, October 2004

PLAYBOY: When was the last time you screamed at an employee?

TRUMP: It might have been two days ago, but it wasn't out of anger; it was a method of getting them to do a better job. Sometimes that works better than honey. I don't actually have a bad temper. I call it controlled violence. I get angry at people for incompetence. I get angry at people who are getting paid a lot of money and don't look sharp when they work for me. That's one reason I do better than everybody else. That's one reason I get more per square foot than other real estate people. That's part of why I'm so successful

Playboy, October 2004

The next Trump book — Decibels: The Secret to His Success

"Because I think a gay man would feel really comfortable buying lemonade from another man."
Playboy, October 2004

I'm not even going to explain that one, I'll just let you enjoy it.

"I nod, and it is done."
Esquire, January 2004

"The day I realized it can be smart to be shallow was, for me, a deep experience."
Trump: Think Like a Billionaire, 2004

"Fighting for the last penny is a very good philosophy to have."
Esquire, January 2004

"If you asked Babe Ruth how he hit home runs, he was unable to tell you. I do things by instinct."
New York Times, September 8, 2004

"For many years I've said that if someone screws you, screw them back. When somebody hurts you, just go after them as viciously and as violently as you can."
How to Get Rich, 2004

"There is something crazy, hot, a phenomenon out there about me, but I'm not sure I can define it and I'm not sure I want to. How do you think 'The Apprentice' would have done if I wasn't a part of it? There are a lot of imitators now and we'll see how they'll do, but I think they'll crash and burn."
New York Times, Sept. 8, 2004

"Other rich people don't do commercials because no one asks them. It's just like 'The Apprentice.' I can't tell you how many of my rich friends are dying, dying to have me put them on that show."
New York Times, Aug. 11, 2004

"I can't help it that I'm a celebrity. What am I going to do, hide under a stone?"
USA Today, Feb. 27, 2004

"... don't let the brevity of these passages prevent you from savouring the profundity of the advice you are about to receive."
How to Get Rich, 2004

"If you don't tell people about your success, they probably won't know about it."
How to Get Rich, 2004

"That's why the banks love me. They love my reputation."
New York Times, March 28, 2004

"The concept of shaking hands is absolutely terrible, and statistically I've been proven right."
Playboy, May, 2004

"[The press] used to think that I was really this horrible, flame-throwing, terrible tyrant. Right? Now I go on a television show, where basically what I do is I fire

41

people, and everyone thinks I'm such a nice guy. Which tells you what a bad image I had."
Larry King Live, May 17, 2005

"Usually, if I fire somebody who's bad, I'll tell them how great they are. Because I don't want to hurt people's feelings."
Larry King Live," May 17, 2005

Exceptions for Rosie, Cher, Ariana Huffington, President Obama, All journalists, Hillary Clinton, the Losers and Haters, Megyn Kelly, every race or nation that is not pillow-case-white, Jon Stewart, war heroes, all women everywhere...

"Some people cast shadows, and other people choose to live in those shadows."
New York Times, Sept. 11, 2005

That's a good quote. I'd say he must have read it somewhere, but we know he doesn't read.

"I think the brand is huge. What is it about me that gets Larry King his highest ratings?"
TrumpNation: The Art of Being The Donald, 2005

The exact same thing that slows traffic as it passes by wreckage.

"If you don't win you can't get away with it. And I win, I win, I always win. In the end, I always win, whether it's in golf, whether it's in tennis, whether it's in life, I just always win. And I tell people I always win, because I do."
TrumpNation: The Art of Being The Donald, 2005

> "The very fact that he's so sensitive about [his fingers] is absolutely hilarious, as is the fact that those notes were apparently written in gold Sharpie, which is so quintessentially Donald Trump: something that gives the passing appearance of wealth, but is really just a cheap tool."
> **—John Oliver**

Why Donald Trump Has Been Sending a Vanity Fair Editor Pictures of His Hands for 25Yrs

The bizarre, decades-long feud between the journalist and the billionaire presidential candidate began when Carter wrote an essay for Spy magazine calling Trump a "short-fingered vulgarian," Carter wrote in this month's editor's letter.

"The most recent offering arrived earlier this year, before his decision to go after the Republican presidential nomination," Carter said in the piece titled "Why Donald Trump Will Always Be a 'Short-Fingered Vulgarian.'"

"Like the other packages, this one included a circled hand and the words, also written in gold Sharpie: 'See, not so short!' I sent the picture back by return mail with a note attached, saying, 'Actually, quite short.'"

Carter wrote that Trump sends "the occasional envelope" of torn-out magazine pages, "On all of them he has circled his hand in gold Sharpie in a valiant effort to highlight the length of his fingers."

People Magazine, October 23, 2016

"A lot of people sit down and discuss their lives, things like are they happy, but it's not like that with me. I don't think positively, I don't think negatively, I just think about the goal. But it's not like I sit down and write goals. I just do things."
Master Apprentice, 2005

"A lot of people build a brand and they study it very carefully and every move is calculated. My moves are not calculated. My moves are totally unalculated ."
TrumpNation: The Art of Being The Donald, 2005

"There's something very seductive about being a television star."
TrumpNation: The Art of Being The Donald, 2005

Yesterday at a conference with Silicon Valley executives, Donald Trump said, "There's nobody like you in the world." Then he put down his mirror and began the meeting.

- Conan O'Brien

"I want a very good-looking guy to play me."
Donald Trump: Master Apprentice, 2005

"If I get my name in the paper, if people pay attention, that's what matters."
Donald Trump: Master Apprentice, 2005

""What really fascinates me is email. I have friends — first of all — half of my friends are under indictment right now because they sent emails to each other about how they're screwing people."
Howard Stern 2005

"How much have I made off the casinos? Off the record, a lot."
Master Apprentice, 2005

On the record, he used shareholder funds to line his pockets, pay personal debt and declared bankruptcy 4 times, defaulted on contracts with his subcontractors — many of whom lost their livelihoods....so, if you call that "making a lot of money off the casino"...then sure.

MEREDITH VIERA: What are you waiting for?

TRUMP: .I hate to say it, I have the No. 1 show on NBC. Is that a correct statement? I mean, The Apprentice is doing great -- The Celebrity Apprentice.

Vieira: What does that have to do....

Trump: It has a lot to do. It sounds so trivial, and I hate to even bring it up, but I'm not allowed to run during the show. You're not allowed to have the show on and be a declared candidate. It's a great show and it's got phenomenal ratings, and until that show is over, I can't declare, because otherwise, NBC would have to take the show off the air, and I think that would be very unfair to NBC.

**The Today Show with Meredith Vieira,
April 7, 2011**

At the time of this statement, The Celebrity Apprentice was 44th in the overall ratings.

"I am a really smart guy."
TIME, April 14, 2011

"My fingers are long and beautiful, as, it has been well documented, are various other parts of my body."
Page Six, April 11, 2011

"A Trump rally being cancelled due to violence is the most predictable thing to happen in this campaign since Donald Trump mentioning the size of his dick."

—John Oliver

"Part of the beauty of me is that I am very rich."
Good Morning America, March 17, 2011

...and the other part is his teeny-tiny girl hands

"It's freezing and snowing in New York – we need global warming!"
Twitter, November 7, 2012

Showcasing both his hilarious grasp of the ironic and his deep understanding for the climate crisis currently facing our planet

"I have never seen a thin person drinking Diet Coke."
Twitter, 2012

"A young rapper named Mac Miller just did a song called 'Donald Trump' and I've just been told it hit over 54 million… 54 million people. I want some money, Mac. Give me some money. I'm entitled to 25% at least. Mac, I want money!"
From the Desk of Donald Trump, 2012

"There have been many bad things said about me over the years, and in some cases they've been true. It doesn't bother me. If I have a fault and somebody exposes that fault or talks about that fault, you won't hear me complain."
The Atlantic, 2013

To quote President Obama, "Oh Come On Man!

"I've won many club championships and I was always the best athlete. But I've won many a club championship. It's something that people don't know unless they are with me and have played with me"
The Atlantic, 2013

"Sorry losers and haters, but my I.Q. is one of the highest -and you all know it! Please don't feel so stupid or insecure, it's not your fault."
Twitter, May 08, 2013

Tomorrow I am going to start a line of "Loser/Hater" towels.

"It's a great building. It's the second-tallest building in Chicago, and I always say it was better for the people of Chicago than it was for Donald Trump."
The Atlantic, 2013

Because it lost a shit-ton of money

"As everybody knows, but the haters & losers refuse to acknowledge, I do not wear a "wig." My hair may not be perfect but it's mine."
Twitter, April 24, 2013

Sounds like he might be tired of being judged based on how he looks.

"My net worth fluctuates, and it goes up and down with markets and with attitudes and with feelings—even my own feelings—but I try."
> **Quoted in The Atlantic, 2013**
> **Lawsuit deposition, 2007**

"Show me someone without an ego, and I'll show you a loser -- having a healthy ego, or high opinion of yourself, is a real positive in life!"
> **Facebook, December 9, 2013**

> *Everything in MODERATION Donald.*

"I've done an incredible job."
> **Atlantic, April 2013**

"I am being proven right about massive vaccinations— the doctors lied. Save our children & their future."
> **Twitter, September 3, 2014**

UNKNOWN FEMALE: Hi. Donald Trump, I have a question for you. I'm here at Georgetown University. And all of us want to know if your hair is real, or it's a toupee or if it's comb-over, dyed amalgamation or mix of one of the above?

KING: One of the most asked questions in America. Let's talk first.

TRUMP: Come on, let's go.

KING: It is not a toupee.

TRUMP: Would you please inform the public.

KING: It is not a toupee. Now, hold on, lean forward a little. No, it's not a toupee. It's not a comb over.

TRUMP: Don't mess it up too much.

KING: It's not a comb over.

TRUMP: It's really not that much of a comb over. I get killed in this hair. I'm getting killed –

KING: Why?

TRUMP: You know the show has gotten great reviews. I've gotten great reviews, everything gotten great reviews, except for one thing, my hair, gets bad reviews.

KING: What do you make of it?

TRUMP: It's a mess.

KING: As long as I've known you've combed it that way. Do comb it?

TRUMP: You know what I do. I take a shower, I wash it, I then comb it and set it and I spray it and it's good for the day, but I'm getting killed on my hair.

KING: Are you thinking, make news here, Donald, changing it?

TRUMP: Well, if I did I think Mark wouldn't let me because the ratings would probably go way down. Do you agree with that Mark? The ratings would go down and he'd say please go back to your old hair style.

KING: So, that's the reason? No personal desire to change it?

TRUMP: I don't care. It's not a big deal. But I don't think so. It's worked.

KING: It's different.

TRUMP: Yes. I don't feel it's even different. It's been the way I've always combed it.
CNN's Larry King Live

> "Donald Trump really has egg on his face now. Which pairs nicely with the hash browns on the top of his head."
>
> —James Corden

"We have a 5 billion dollar website. I have so many websites ... I hire people. They do a website. It costs me three dollars."
Trump Tower, June 16, 2015

"I have a total net worth and now with the increase it will be well over $10 billion, but here total net worth of $8 billion. Net worth—not assets, not liabilities—a net worth. ... I'm not doing that to brag. Because you know what? I don't have to brag. I don't have to. Believe it or not."
New York City, June 16, 2015

"I do whine because I want to win, and I'm not happy about not winning, and I am a whiner, and I keep whining and whining until I win."
CNN, Aug. 10, 2015

"What I say is what I say."
Republican presidential debate, Aug. 6, 2015

"I would like to wish everyone, including all haters and losers (of which, sadly, there are many) a truly happy and enjoyable Memorial Day!"
Twitter, May 24 2015

"I don't look forward or not look forward."
Washington Post, July 12, 2015

"I'm really rich."
New Yorker, June 16, 2015

"Americans like Trump because he's got loads of money, which is sort of their version of being clever. He's all over the news, even though he looks weird. Like a guinea pig staring at you through the porthole on a washing machine."
—Barry Shitpeas

In an audio clip, recently obtained by The Washington Post, is a 1991 interview between a People magazine reporter and a man who calls himself "John Miller."

The recording was unearthed by Post reporter Mark Fisher.

"There is a certain voice, a certain cadence, a certain rhythm, a certain speech mannerism that are very distinctly Trumpy," Fisher told Inside Edition. "There are at least a half-a-dozen editors and reporters that got these calls on a regular basis from him. We do not have an exact number but it seems it is something he did regularly. We also spoke to some of his former executives that say they heard him in his office making those calls."

In 1991, Carswell was suspicious that "John Miller" was in fact, Trump posing as a publicist. The reporter even played the tape for Marla Maples, who reportedly burst into tears and confirmed that the man on the tape was her boyfriend.
As news of the recording broke, Trump quickly went on the defensive.

**Marc Fisher and Will Hobson,
The Washington Post,
May 13 2016**

"My life has been about winning. My life has not been about losing."
Time, August 20, 2015

Apparently, your life has been about whining, not winning.

"We need a leader that wrote The Art of the Deal."
New York City, June 16, 2015

> "Many thanks Donald Trump for suggesting I run for President, based on the fact that I wrote 'The Art of the Deal.'
> **— Tony Schwartz**
> **Twitter, June 16, 2016**

"Let's say I was worth $10. People would say, 'Who the [expletive] are you?' You understand? They know my statement. Fortune. My book, The Art of the Deal, based on my fortune. If I didn't make a fortune, who the [expletive] is going to buy The Art of the Deal? That's why they watched 'The Apprentice.' Because of my great success."
Washington Post, July 12, 2015

"I went to an Ivy League school. I'm very highly educated. I know words, I have the best words…"
Hilton Head, December 30, 2015

"@ilduce2016: "It is better to live one day as a lion than 100 years as a sheep." – @realDonaldTrump #MakeAmericaGreatAgain"
Twitter, February 28, 2016

Always a bad sign when the Republican front-runner takes to quoting Mussolini.

> "He's always calling me 'Little Marco' … and I'll admit he's taller than me, he's 6'2" which is why I don't understand why he has hands the size of someone who's 5'2". Have you seen his hands? You know what they say about men with small hands."
>
> **– Marco Rubio**

"Look at those hands, are they small hands? And, [Republican rival Marco Rubio] referred to my hands: 'If they're small, something else must be small.' I guarantee you there's no problem. I guarantee."
GOP Debate, March 3, 2016

> "Donald Trump just talked about his dick during a presidential debate! A dick which I presume looks like a Cheeto with the cheese dust rubbed off."
> – **John Oliver**

"We have losers. We have losers. We have people that don't have it."
Trump Tower, June 16, 2015

"People say, Mr. Trump, you're not a nice person. But actually I am a nice person. I think I'm very nice."
Trump Tower, June 16, 2015

"I don't think I've made mistakes. Every time somebody said I made a mistake, they do the polls and my numbers go up, so I guess I haven't made any mistakes."
Iowa State Fair, August 15, 2015

"I had some beautiful pictures taken in which I had a big smile on my face. I looked happy, I looked content, I looked like a very nice person, which in theory I am."
Crippled America: How to Make America Great Again, 2015

"I think apologizing's a great thing, but you have to be wrong. I will absolutely apologize, sometime in the hopefully distant future, if I'm ever wrong."
The Tonight Show with Jimmy Fallon, September 2015

At the Family Leadership Summit in Ames, Iowa, Moderator Frank Luntz asked Trump whether he has ever asked God for forgiveness for his actions.

"I am not sure I have. I just go on and try to do a better job from there. I don't think so; I think if I do something wrong, I think, I just try and make it right. I don't bring God into that picture. I don't."

Trump said that while he hasn't asked God for forgiveness, he does participate in Holy Communion.

"When I drink my little wine -- which is about the only wine I drink -- and have my little cracker, I guess that is a form of asking for forgiveness, and I do that as often as possible because I feel cleansed."
July 18, 2015

"I think I am, actually humble. I think I'm much more humble than you would understand."
60 Minutes interview, July 17, 2016

"Trump Steaks, where are the steaks? Do we have steaks? We have Trump Steaks."
NY Press Conference, March 8, 2016

At this press conference, Donald presented reporters with a range of "Trump" products, most of which are defunct businesses that failed. There was Trump water, Trump magazine, Trump Vodka, Trump Steaks and Trump wine...(Actually, Trump Wine is still in business, but it is not affiliated with him) The steaks went out of business in 2007, what he supplied at the conference were Bush Bros. Steaks. He also vowed to start Trump University back up "after the lawsuits."

"Over the years, his name has been on some things that have arguably been very un-good, including Trump Shuttle, which no longer exists; Trump Vodka, which was discontinued; Trump Magazine, which folded; Trump World Magazine, which also folded; Trump University, over which he's being sued; and of course, the travel-booking site GoTrump.com, whose brief existence was, I imagine, a real thorn in the side of anyone hoping GotRump.com featured a single thing worth masturbating to."

—John Oliver

TRUMP
FAMILY MAN

"There's not a lot of disagreement because, ultimately, Ivana does exactly as I tell her to do."

"To tell you the truth, I've made Ivana a very popular woman. I've made a lot of satellites. Hey, whether it's Marla or Ivana. Marla can do any movie she wants to now. Ivana can do whatever she wants,"
Vanity Fair, September 1990

"I want five children, like in my own family, because with five, then I will know that one will be guaranteed to turn out like me,"
Vanity Fair, 1990

"My father is a very hardworking guy, and that's his focus in life, so I got a lot of the paternal attention that a boy wants and needs from my grandfather."
--Donald Trump Jr.

"Statistically, my children have a very bad shot. Children of successful people are generally very, very troubled, not successful. They don't have the right shtick. You never know until they're tested. But I do well with my children."
Playboy, March 1990

"My marriage, it seemed, was the only area of my life in which I was willing to accept something less than perfection."
Surviving at the Top, 1990

"I knew from the start that Ivana was different from just about all of the other women I'd been spending time with. Good looks had been my top — and sometimes, to be honest, my only — priority in my man-about-town days. Ivana was gorgeous, but she was also ambitious and intelligent. When I introduced her to friends and associates, I said, "Believe me. This one's different." Everyone knew what I meant, and I think everyone sensed that I found the combination of beauty and brains almost unbelievable. I suppose I was a little naive, and perhaps, like a lot of men, I had been taught by Hollywood that one woman couldn't have both."
Trump: Surviving at the Top, 1990

> Donald took Ivana to Aspen, Colo., not knowing her Olympian status. She feigned altitude sickness while Donald, a ski novice, took a lesson.
>
> "Sure enough, 10 minutes later I was on the mountains and looking at him doing full turns, and it was not fun," says Ivana.
>
> "The second day, he was getting good. So he said, 'Ivana, let's go ski.' I asked the instructor to put the ski boots on me like a beginner. Donald was like, 'OK, darling, you can do it!' I took off and he got so angry. He said, 'I will never [ski] again for anybody! Even Ivana!' So I play for his ego."
>
> **New York Post, April 3, 2016**

"I'm not a great believer in always trying to work things out, because it just doesn't happen that way.

The Art of the Comeback, 1990

"I would never buy Ivana any decent jewels or pictures. Why give her negotiable assets?"

Vanity Fair, September 1990

> "How can you say you love us? You don't love us! You don't even love yourself. You just love your money."
> **-- Donald Trump Jr., then 12 years old, as reported in a Vanity Fair**

"I don't like the concept of divorce, but sometimes it becomes necessary"

The Larry King Show, 1990

"When a man leaves a woman, especially when it was perceived that he has left for a piece of ass—a good one! — there are 50 percent of the population who will love the woman who was left."

Vanity Fair, September 1990

*Two years **before** Donald left Ivana for his mistress Marla Maples.*

In September 1994, a little less than a year after Tiffany was born to Trump and his second wife, Marla Maples, the couple appeared on an episode of Lifestyles of the Rich and Famous.

"Donald, what does Tiffany have of yours and what does Tiffany have of Marla's?" asked host Robin Leach.

"She's a very beautiful baby," Trump replied. "She's got Marla's legs. We don't know whether or not"—he put his hands to his chest [and cupped them] to indicate breasts—"she's got this part yet, but time will tell."
Mother Jones, July 27, 2016

Even his infant daughter is just another future set of tits.

"I think that putting a wife to work is a very dangerous thing. If you're in business for yourself, I really think it's a bad idea to put your wife working for you. I think it's a really bad idea. I think that was the single greatest cause of what happened to my marriage with Ivana."
Primetime Live, March 10 1994

Trump began reminiscing about one of his well-publicized breakups with Marla. "She was very hurt," he said. "Michael Bolton calls Marla and says, 'Marla, I'd like to take you out.' And he falls madly in love with her. Now, I say to myself, Wait a minute. I don't like this. Michael Bolton—he's got the No. 1 fucking album in the world, Time, Love and Tenderness, and what that does to a guy like me, a competitive guy, it's like an affirmation that the girl has to be great, because the No. 1 singer has fallen for her. There's nothing wrong with what she's doing. I left her. Not only that. I left her like a dog.

"So what happens is, I say, 'What the fuck is going on?' I do a Trump number on her. All-enveloping. I call her. She says, 'How could you have left me the way you did?' She decides to go to Hawaii with me instead of to Europe with Michael Bolton. In Maui, this guy finds out where we are, and starts sending flowers. Yellow roses with a note: 'I've got Georgia on my mind. Love, Michael.' She's torn. I've left her twice. But she drops him and comes back to me."

Vanity Fair, March 1990

> It was that love of women that led to the couple's divorce. Ivana discovered that her husband was cheating on her with former beauty queen Marla Maples. As Ivana told Barbara Walters in a 1991 "20/20" interview, Maples stopped her at a restaurant in Aspen and told her, "I'm Marla and I love your husband. Do you?"
>
> **New York Post, April 3, 2016**

"The most difficult aspect of the prenuptial agreement is informing your future wife (or husband): I love you very much, but just in case things don't work out, this is what you will get in the divorce. There are basically three types of women and reactions. One is the good woman who very much loves her future husband, solely for himself, but refuses to sign the agreement on principle. I fully understand this, but the man should take a pass anyway and find someone else. The other is the calculating woman who refuses to sign the prenuptial agreement because she is expecting to take advantage of the poor, unsuspecting sucker she's got in her grasp. There is also the woman who will openly and quickly sign a prenuptial agreement in order to make a quick hit and take the money given to her."

TRUMP: The Art of the Comeback, 1997

"For a man to be successful he needs support at home, just like my father had from my mother, not someone who is always griping and bitching. When a man has to endure a woman who is not supportive and complains constantly about his not being home enough or not being attentive enough, he will not be very successful unless he is unable to cut the cord."

TRUMP: The Art of the Comeback, 1997

Trump Family Values

In 2000, Donald and his relatives were feuding over the details of his father's will; Fred Sr.'s company had been providing health insurance to Fred Jr.'s family, which included Donald's nephew's son, who had cerebral palsy. After Sr.'s death, Donald informed the insurer that benefits were to continue, as needed…but, when Jr.'s family disputed the will, Trump cut off the medical benefits that were paying for the medical care of his nephew's ill son — all to gain leverage in the lawsuit.

The New York Daily News

"I don't know why, but I seem to bring out either the best or worst in women."
TRUMP: The Art of the Comeback, 1997
"I grew up in a very normal family. I was always of the opinion that aggression, sex drive, and everything that goes along with it was on the man's part of the table, not the woman's."
TRUMP: The Art of the Comeback, 1997

""You know who's one of the great beauties of the world—according to everybody—and I helped create her? Ivanka. My daughter, Ivanka. She's 6 feet tall, she's got the best body. She made a lot of money as a model—a tremendous amount. She's considered one of the most beautiful women. And she really is, she's a *great* beauty."
The Howard Stern Show, 2003

"Every guy in the country wants to go out with my daughter."
New York magazine, Dec. 13, 2004

"She does have a very nice figure. I've said that if Ivanka weren't my daughter, perhaps I'd be dating her."
The View, March 6, 2006

"It would be really disappointing — not really — but it would depend on what's inside the magazine. I don't think Ivanka would do that, although she does have a very nice figure. I've said if Ivanka weren't my daughter, perhaps I'd be dating her."
The View, March 7, 2006

On the hypothetical prospect of Ivanka posing for Playboy..."disappointing — not really..." EEE Gads Dad!

> "I remember skiing with him and we were racing. I was ahead, and he reached his ski pole out and pulled me back."
> --Ivanka Trump

"Yeah, she's really something, and what a beauty, that one. If I weren't happily married and, ya know, her father ..."
Rolling Stone, September 2015

HOWARD STERN: By the way, your daughter,"

TRUMP: "She's beautiful,"

STERN: "Can I say this? A piece of ass,"

TRUMP: "Yeah,"
The Howard Stern Show, September, 2004

[Wendy] Williams introduced a question-and-answer game called 'Fave Five', a regular feature on the show when Trump appeared with his daughter.

She asks: 'Ivanka, what's the favorite thing you have in common with your father?', who replies with: 'Either real estate or golf.'

When she puts the same questions to Trump, he answers: 'Well, I was going to say sex, but I can't relate that to her', pointing to Ivanka.

The Wendy Williams Show, 2013

The Daily Mail, UK

According to a report from MSNBC Wednesday, Donald Trump told Dr. Oz in a pre-taped interview how much he loves kissing his daughter Ivanka Trump.

"Dr. Oz said when Ivanka Trump came on stage, 'It's nice to see a dad kiss his daughter,'" reported NBC's Peter Alexander. "Trump responded that he kisses her every chance he gets."

MSNBC, September 14, 2016

"If he wasn't my father, I would spray him with Mace."

— Ivanka Trump
The Chicago Tribune, August 24, 2006

"I mean, I won't do anything to take care of them. I'll supply funds and she'll take care of the kids. It's not like I'm gonna be walking the kids down Central Park. Well, Marla used to say, 'I can't believe you're not walking Tiffany down the street,' you know, in a carriage. Right, I'm gonna be walking down Fifth Avenue with a baby in a carriage. It just didn't work."

The Howard Stern Show, 2005

"When a lawyer facing Trump in 2011 asked for a break to pump breastmilk for her infant daughter, Donald reacted very poorly. 'He got up, his face got red, he shook his finger at me and he screamed, 'You're disgusting, you're disgusting,' and he ran out of there,' attorney Elizabeth Beck told CNN. "

Trump's attorney does not dispute that his client called Beck "disgusting."

CNN, July 29, 2015

"If you have the money, having children is great."

Larry King Live, May 17, 2005

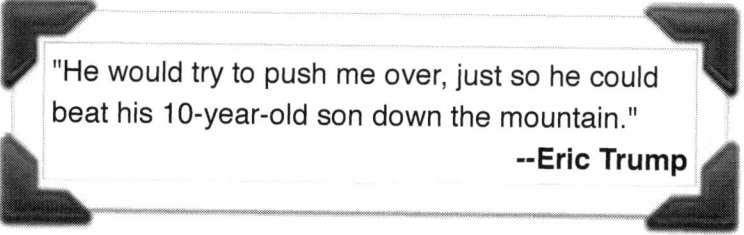

"He would try to push me over, just so he could beat his 10-year-old son down the mountain."

--Eric Trump

"There was a great softness to Ivana, and she still has that softness, but during this period of time, she became an executive, not a wife...

TrumpNation, 2005

You know, I don't want to sound too much like a chauvinist, but when I come home and dinner's not ready, I'll go through the roof, okay?"

TrumpNation, 2005

"I don't [change diapers]. It's not my thing. You know what, I'm a good father but that's not my thing and Melania's going to be a great mother. To a large extent it's up to the women. There are a lot of women out there who, you know, demand the husband act like the wife and there are a lot of husbands who listen to that."

Opie and Anthony, 2006

"In a way, [my brother, Donald Jr.] raised me. My father, I love and I appreciate, but he always worked 24 hours a day."

--Eric Trump, 2006

"Pregnancy is never, um, a wonderful thing for the woman, it's a wonderful thing for the husband, it's certainly an inconvenience for a business. And whether people want to say that or not, the fact is it is an inconvenience for a person that is running a business."

Dateline, October 3, 2004

"I'll tell you what I've learned: Children are tough. Much tougher than people think. ... I'm a really good father, but not a really good husband. You've probably figured out my children really like me--love me--a lot. (...) The hardest thing for me about raising kids has been finding the time. I know friends who leave their business so they can spend more time with their children, and I say, 'Gimme a break!' My children could not love me more if I spent fifteen times more time with them."

--Donald Trump

"She's not giving me 100 percent. She's giving me 84 percent, and 16 percent is going towards taking care of children."
TIME, May 23, 2011

On the problem with hiring mothers...

"Actually, I was only kidding. You can get that baby out of here. Don't worry, I think she really believed me that I love having a baby crying while I'm speaking. That's O.K. People don't understand. That's O.K."
Campaign Rally, August 2, 2016

Donald Trump, booting a mother and her crying baby from a rally moments after saying "I love babies"

"I'm very proud, because Don and Eric and Ivanka — and you know, to a lesser extent because she just got out of school, out of college— but Tiffany who has also been so terrific. They work so hard."
Fox & Friends, November 8, 2016

"lesser extent" — ouch

TRUMP

PERVERT-IN-CHIEF

STERN: So you treat women with respect?
TRUMP: I can't say that...

Definition of Perversion
1) the action of perverting : the condition of being perverted
2) a perverted form; especially : an aberrant sexual practice or interest especially when habitual

Definition of Aberrant

1) diverting from the normal or accepted practice.

Peppered throughout the chapter, I have included fifteen boxes that briefly describe alleged sexual assaults, mostly in the accuser's own words. Starting with the Pussygate transcript, where Donald can do anything he wants — even grabbing women by the pussy, because he's a celebrity — puts all that comes afterwards into perspective.

This is a small man...and I mean in every way. Everything, from his disproportionately tiny hands (a likely predictor that he has a wee penis) to his bloated orange gob, crooked slobbering maw, and dainty little princess feet, this is a man who oozes sleaze from every pore.

> "NBC suspended Billy Bush for his words on the Trump tape, which means there is currently a higher standard for host for the third hour of the Today show than there is for the Republican nominee for president."
> —Seth Meyers

PUSSY-GATE

"Following is an unedited transcript of the tape in which Donald J. Trump repeatedly made vulgar comments about women. Mr. Trump was filmed talking to the television personality Billy Bush of "Access Hollywood" on the set of "Days of Our Lives," where Mr. Trump was making a cameo appearance. They are later joined by the actress

Arianne Zucker. The transcription is by Penn Bullock of The New York Times."

Donald J. Trump: You know and ...

Unknown: She used to be great. She's still very beautiful.

Trump: I moved on her, actually. You know, she was down on Palm Beach. I moved on her, and I failed. I'll admit it.

Unknown: Whoa.

Trump: I did try and fuck her. She was married.

Unknown: That's huge news.

Trump: No, no, Nancy. No, this was [unintelligible] — and I moved on her very heavily. In fact, I took her out furniture shopping.

She wanted to get some furniture. I said, "I'll show you where they have some nice furniture." I took her out furniture —

I moved on her like a bitch. But I couldn't get there. And she was married. Then all of a sudden I see her, she's now got the big phoney tits and everything. She's totally changed her look.

Billy Bush: Sheesh, your girl's hot as shit. In the purple.

Trump: Whoa! Whoa!

Bush: Yes! The Donald has scored. Whoa, my man!

[Crosstalk]

Trump: Look at you, you are a pussy.

[Crosstalk]

Trump: All right, you and I will walk out.

[Silence]

Trump: Maybe it's a different one.

Bush: It better not be the publicist. No, it's, it's her, it's …

Trump: Yeah, that's her. With the gold. I better use some Tic Tacs just in case I start kissing her. You know, I'm automatically attracted to beautiful — I just start kissing them. It's like a magnet. Just kiss. I don't even wait. *And when you're a star, they let you do it. You can do anything.*

Bush: Whatever you want.

Trump: *Grab 'em by the pussy. You can do anything.*

Bush: Uh, yeah, those legs, all I can see is the legs.

Trump: Oh, it looks good.

Bush: Come on shorty.

Trump: Ooh, nice legs, huh?

Bush: Oof, get out of the way, honey. Oh, that's good legs. Go ahead.

Trump: It's always good if you don't fall out of the bus. Like Ford, Gerald Ford, remember?

Bush: Down below, pull the handle.

Trump: Hello, how are you? Hi!

Arianne Zucker: Hi, Mr. Trump. How are you? Pleasure to meet you.

Trump: Nice seeing you. Terrific, terrific. You know Billy Bush?

Bush: Hello, nice to see you. How you doing, Arianne?

Zucker: Doing very well, thank you. Are you ready to be a soap star?

Trump: We're ready, let's go. Make me a soap star.

Bush: How about a little hug for the Donald? He just got off the bus.

Zucker: Would you like a little hug, darling?

Trump: O.K., absolutely. Melania said this was O.K.

Bush: How about a little hug for the Bushy? I just got off the bus.

Zucker: Bushy, Bushy.

Bush: Here we go. Excellent. Well, you've got a nice co-star here.

Zucker: Yes, absolutely.

Trump: Good. After you.

[Break in video]

Trump: Come on, Billy, don't be shy.

Bush: Soon as a beautiful woman shows up, he just, he takes off. This always happens.

Trump: Get over here, Billy.

Zucker: I'm sorry, come here.

Bush: Let the little guy in here, come on.

Zucker: Yeah, let the little guy in. How you feel now? Better? I should actually be in the middle.

Bush: It's hard to walk next to a guy like this.

Zucker: Here, wait, hold on.

Bush: Yeah, you get in the middle, there we go.

Trump: Good, that's better.

Zucker: This is much better. This is —

Trump: That's better.

Zucker: [Sighs]

Bush: Now, if you had to choose honestly between one of us. Me or the Donald?

Trump: I don't know, that's tough competition.

Zucker: That's some pressure right there.

Bush: Seriously, if you had — if you had to take one of us as a date.

Zucker: I have to take the Fifth on that one.

Bush: Really?

Zucker: Yup — I'll take both.

Trump: Which way?

Zucker: Make a right. Here we go. [inaudible]

Bush: Here he goes. I'm gonna leave you here.

Trump: O.K.

Bush: Give me my microphone.

Trump: O.K. Oh, you're finished?

Bush: You're my man, yeah.

Trump: Oh, good.

NBC Parking Lot, September 2005

> "The microphones, I mean to be honest should, you know, should never have been on."
> —**Donald Trump**
> **EWTN, October 27, 2016**

> **Allegation No. 1**
> **He was like an octopus...**
>
> **Early 1980s:** Jessica Leeds told The New York Times that Donald Trump groped her in First Class shortly after their flight took off to New York. Trump raised the armrest and grabbed her breasts and tried to put his hand up her skirt. "He was like an octopus; His hands were everywhere," she said.

"I've never had any trouble in bed, but if I'd had affairs with half the starlets and female athletes the newspapers linked me with, I'd have no time to breathe."
Surviving at the Top, 1990

> "You've ruined more models' lives than bulimia. You've disappointed more women than Sex and the City 2."
>
> **—Lisa Lampanelli**

"You know, it doesn't really matter what [the media] write as long as you've got a young and beautiful piece of ass."
Esquire, 1991

> **Allegation No. 2**
> **As a woman, I felt violated…**
>
> **1989:** Ivana Trump said in a court deposition about their divorce that Donald Trump "violated" her during sex following a violent attack. She reportedly described the attack as rape. She later recanted saying "As a woman, I felt violated, as the love and tenderness, which he normally exhibited towards me, was absent. I referred to this as a 'rape,' but I do not want my words to be interpreted in a literal or criminal sense."

TRUMP: [Women]You have to treat 'em like shit.

PHILIP JOHNSON: You'd make a good mafioso.

TRUMP: One of the greatest.
        New York magazine, Nov. 9, 1992

Trump "boasts about having poured a whole bottle of wine down Marie Brenner's back after she wrote a story on him that he hated," *New York* magazine reported in 1992.

"Well, it wasn't a bottle, actually—it was a glass," Brenner told The Daily Beast on Saturday. "I didn't even notice it was happening, because like everything with Donald, it was a stealth maneuver. It came from behind."

"It was a black jacket, so I'm still waiting for him to replace it," she chuckled.

The Daily Beast, August 8, 2015

HOST (voice-over): "One of the leaders to keep Tyson out of prison is Donald Trump, the casino owner, who could lose millions if Tyson is unable to fight at his resorts."

TRUMP: "It's my opinion that to a large extent, Mike Tyson was railroaded in this case."

HOST (voice-over): "Tyson's victim, Deisree Washington, went public almost immediately after the verdict. She is on the cover of 'People' magazine and tonight on ABC 20/20 broadcast, she will say that she was offered a million dollars to drop the rape charge against Tyson."

TRUMP: "You have a young woman that was in his hotel room late in the evening at her own will. You have a young woman seen dancing for the beauty contest—dancing with a big smile on her face, looked happy as can be."
        NBC News, February 21, 1992

> "On Monday, former heavyweight champ Mike Tyson endorsed Donald Trump. Tyson joins Trump's biggest group of supporters: people who have been hit in the head a lot."
> —**Conan O'Brien**

Allegation No. 3
Without introducing himself...

Early 1990s: Kristin Anderson claimed that Trump touched her vagina at The China Club in Manhattan, without introducing himself or speaking to her, when he reached his hand up her skirt while they were seated. "This is the vivid part for me: The person on my right, unbeknownst to me was Donald Trump, put their hands up my skirt. He did touch my vagina through my underwear, absolutely."

"I think that putting a wife to work is a very dangerous thing. If you're in business for yourself, I really think it's a bad idea to put your wife working for you"
ABC's Primetime Live, March 10, 1994

COLLINS: So why in 1992 did you tell a writer for New York magazine, Marie Brenner, that 'You have to treat women like shit" — ultimately pouring a bottle of wine down her back?

TRUMP: I didn't say that. The woman's a liar, extremely unattractive, lots of problems because of her looks.

COLLINS: That statement is exactly why women think you're a chauvinist pig.

TRUMP: They're right — and not. People say, "How can you say such a thing?" but there's a truth in it, in a modified form. Psychologists will tell you that some women want to be treated with respect, others differently. I tell friends who treat their wives magnificently, get treated like crap in return, "Be rougher and you'll see a different relationship.' Unfortunately, with people in general, you get more with vinegar than honey.
Primetime Live, 1994

> "Yesterday, Donald Trump tweeted that millions of people voted illegally on Election Day. Then someone told Trump it's not illegal for women to vote."
>
> —**Conan O'Brien**

"I have days where I think it's great," [Marla working] "And then I have days where, if I come home — and I don't want to sound too much like a chauvinist — but when I come home and dinner's not ready, I go through the roof."
ABC's Primetime Live, March 10, 1994

"I love creating stars. And to a certain extent, I've done that with Ivana. To a certain extent, I've done that with Marla. And I like that...Unfortunately, after they're a star, the fun is over for me. It's like a creation process. It's almost like creating a building; it's pretty sad."
ABC's Primetime Live, March 10, 1994

"I don't know why, but I seem to bring out either the best or worst in women."
Trump:The Art of the Comeback, 1997

> **Accusation No. 4**
> **And tried to get up my dress again.**
>
> **1993:** Makeup artist Jill Harth accuses Trump of cornering her and groping her in his daughter Ivanka's bedroom. "He pushed me up against the wall, and had his hands all over me and tried to get up my dress again," Harth told The Guardian, "and I had to physically say: 'What are you doing? Stop it.' It was a shocking thing to have him do this because he knew I was with George [Harth's boyfriend at the time], he knew they were in the next room. And how could he be doing this when I'm there for business?"

"There's nothing I love more than women, but they're really a lot different than portrayed. They are far worse than men, far more aggressive, and boy, can they be smart. Let's give credit where credit is due, and let's salute women for their tremendous power, which most men are afraid to admit they have."
Trump: The Art of the Comeback, 1997

"I grew up in a very normal family. I was always of the opinion that aggression, sex drive, and everything that goes along with it was on the man's part of the table, not the woman's.
Trump: The Art of the Comeback, 1997

As I grew older and witnessed life firsthand from a front-row seat at the great clubs, social events, and parties of the world — I have seen just about everything — I began to realize that women are far stronger than men. Their sex drive makes us look like babies. Some women try to portray themselves as being of the weaker sex, but don't believe it for a minute."

Trump: The Art of the Comeback, 1997

"I remember attending a magnificent dinner being given by one of the most admired people in the world. I was seated next to a lady of great social pedigree and wealth. Her husband was sitting on the other side of the table, and we were having a very nice but extremely straight conversation. All of a sudden I felt her hand on my knee, then on my leg. She started petting me in all different ways. I looked at her and asked, 'Is everything all right?' I didn't want to make a scene in a ballroom full of five hundred VIPs. The amazing part about her was who she was — one of the biggest of the big. She

then asked me to dance, and I accepted. While we were dancing she became very aggressive, and I said, 'Look, we have a problem. Your husband is sitting at the table, and so is my wife.'

'Donald,' she said. 'I don't care. I just don't care. I have to have you, and I have to have you now.' I told her that I'd call her, but that she had to stop the behaviour immediately. She made me promise, and I did. When I called I just called to say hello, and that was the end of that.

But the level of aggression was unbelievable. This is not infrequent, it happens all the time."
Trump: The Art of the Comeback, 1997

I just threw up a little.

"I love women. They've come into my life. They've gone out of my life. Even those who have exited somewhat ungracefully still have a place in my heart. I only have one regret in the women department -- that I never had the opportunity to court Lady Diana Spencer. I met her on a number of occasions."
Trump:The Art of the Comeback, 1997

STERN: Why do people think it's egotistical of you to say you could've gotten with Lady Di? You could've gotten her, right? You could've nailed her.

TRUMP: I think I could have.
The Howard Stern Show, 1997

Donald Trump turned up Monday for a carol sing by a youth choir outside Manhattan's Plaza Hotel. He asked two of the girls how old they were. After they replied they were 14, Trump said, "Wow! Just think — in a couple years I'll be dating you.

**Chicago Tribune, December 1992
(Trump was 46 at the time)**

"If I told the real stories of my experiences with women, often seemingly very happily married and important women, this book would be a guaranteed best-seller (which it will be anyway!). I'd love to tell all, using names and places, but I just don't think it's right."
Trump: The Art of the Comeback, 1997

TRUMP: The Miss Universe, it turns out, the woman who won last year, blows up to a fat pig. I mean, like obese. We whipped this fat slob into shape.

STERN: I don't know how you did it. I see all these diet plans, everything else. God bless you. You whipped her into shape, and you held the whole pageant together. Congratulations.

TRUMP: Well, that was an amazing one. She went from 118 to almost 170.

STERN: And you got her right down again to 118, didn't you?

TRUMP: Well, she's going to be there. She's probably 145 or something. She gained about 55 pounds in a period of nine months. She was like an eating machine. What does a girl eat in less than a year to gain [55 pounds]?
Howard Stern Show, February 1, 1997

> "Trump's performance-art character is butch in the sense that certain gay icons are butch — bikers, cowboys, and the rest of the Village People — and appealing to certain men for similar reasons, one of which is overcompensation for threats against their virility."
> **—Kevin Williamson**

"Women have one of the great acts of all time. The smart ones act very feminine and needy, but inside they are real killers. The person who came up with the expression 'the weaker sex' was either very naive or had to be kidding. I have seen women manipulate men with just a twitch of their eye — or perhaps another body part."
Trump: The Art of the Comeback, 1997

HOWARD STERN: So you'll just have straight intercourse with a rubber with them right?

TRUMP: Well, I don't know, you know there's lots of different ways of doing it. It's a very complicated subject. They say that more people were killed by women in this act than killed in Vietnam, OK.

STERN: Yes, that is true.

TRUMP: You know, you get criticized for that statement, but that statement is very easily true.

STERN: I even went as far to say that you're braver than any Vietnam vet because you're out there screwing a lot of women.

TRUMP: Getting the Congressional Medal of Honor, in actuality.
    Howard Stern Show, May 7, 1998

TRUMP: You won't find rocket scientists, you won't find brain surgeons. What you'll find are the most beautiful women in the world.

STERN: And they do wear bikinis and thongs, right?

TRUMP: They wear thongs, they wear bikinis, they wear high heels. They wear just about everything that you're not supposed to wear because that's not politically correct.

STERN: Right, the show is totally politically incorrect.

TRUMP: Totally politically incorrect; You know, Miss America went to politically correct and their ratings have been nose-diving. They're not allowed to wear heels. They're not allowed to wears shoes. They have to wear these very large bathing suits in one piece. We don't do that.

The problem with Miss America, you know the girls are talented, they do have talent, but it's very tough to find great beauty with great talent, and they do. And I'm a big fan of Miss America, I think it's great, I literally host it in Atlantic City because of my places. But, I'll tell you the women in Miss America are just not nearly as beautiful as the women in Miss USA or Miss Universe.

STERN: Hey, I'm gonna tell you something, maybe you can't say it, I will. In Miss America, a lot of them are pigs. They're flat.

TRUMP: Well, it's a different level of standard and it's a different level of beauty.

Howard Stern Show, May 7, 1998

> "It is a little ironic that the Miss USA beauty pageant is overseen by one of the ugliest souls on the planet."
> —**John Oliver**

TRUMP: See, I would never want to date a Miss Universe during a run, but after your reign, I take them out to dinner.

STERN: You do them.
Howard Stern Show, May 7, 1998

HOWARD STERN: I'm not tuning in for a debate. I don't want any brainy broads. I want a hot looking chick. When I go to the beach, at Jones Beach, I can see hotter chicks than I see on Miss America. That's why this Miss Universe is good. I'm with Donald on this. He knows what guys dig: thongs, high heels.

ROBIN QUIVERS: You want to see pretty women.

STERN: Pretty, dumb chicks.

TRUMP: You know, we don't base it on talent. Hey Robin, we don't base it on talent, we don't base it on brains. We don't base it—we base it on one thing: beauty.

STERN: As Donald once said to me off the air, I wanna be able to watch this thing with the sound off, don't even matter. I wanna hear conversation I'll talk to my wife. You know what I'm saying?

TRUMP: That's exactly right.
Howard Stern Show, May 7, 1998

"Women are worse than men, they're more sexually aggressive than men; If they're married they're even worse."
Howard Stern Show, May 7, 1998

HOWARD STERN: Have you had sex with Anna Nicole Smith?

TRUMP: It's funny Howard, if I had sex with a number of women that I'm supposed to have had sex with, I wouldn't be talking to you right now. I'd be dead,

STERN: Yeah, you'd be dead. You'd have some disease.
TRUMP: I'd be dead.
    Howard Stern Show, May 7, 1998

"I think the only difference between me and the other candidates is that I'm more honest and my women are more beautiful."
    New York Times, 1999

"I go out with the most beautiful women in the world. Certain guys tell me they want women of substance, not beautiful models. It just means they can't get beautiful models."
    Maureen Dowd, New York Times, 1999

A New Hampshire state rep got in trouble for calling women, "vaginas." Can you imagine referring to some by their genitals? What a dick!
    — Conan O'Brien

"Nice tits, no brains"
Howard Stern Show, 1999

On his spouse, Marla Maples, shortly after they separated

"There are those that say that if President Clinton was caught with a supermodel, he would have been everyone's hero. Now, of course, I would never say a thing like that, but there are those that say that."
Howard Stern Show, November 9, 1999

"I never thought she was good-looking. I don't think she's got good skin. I don't think she's got a great face. I think her lips are too big, to be honest with you, they look like too big."
Howard Stern Show, 2000

On Angelina Jolie

"Now, somebody who a lot of people don't give credit to but in actuality is really beautiful is Paris Hilton."

"I've known Paris Hilton from the time she's 12. Her parents are friends of mine, and, you know, the first time I saw her, she walked into the room and I said, 'Who the hell is that?'

Stern then asked Trump if he wanted "to bang her".

She's a very... Well, at 12 I wasn't interested. I've never been into that. They've sort of always stuck around that 25 category.
The Howard Stern Show, 2003

> Then it was revealed - from Trump to Stern - that he had watched Paris Hilton's sex tape.
>
> When asked what he thought of the tape, he said he thought it "probably made Paris even better".

"With the proper woman you don't need Viagra"
The Howard Stern Show, 2004

"Frankly, I wouldn't mind if there were an anti-Viagra, something with the opposite effect. I'm not

bragging. I'm just lucky. I don't need it. I've always said, "If you need Viagra, you're probably with the wrong girl."
Playboy, October 2004

TRUMP: There's something there, right? But you have to like freckles. I've seen a — you know, a close-up of her chest, and a lot of freckles. Are you into freckles?

STERN: Can you imagine the sex with this troubled [woman]?

TRUMP: You're probably right. She's probably deeply troubled, and therefore great in bed. How come the deeply troubled women, you know, deeply, deeply troubled, they're always the best in bed? (…) You don't want to be with 'em for the long term; But for the short term, there's nothing like it.
Howard Stern Show December 14, 2004

A 58 year old Trump discussing sex with 20-something Lindsay Lohan…I'm troubled.

"All of the women on The Apprentice flirted with me — consciously or unconsciously. That's to be expected."
How to Get Rich, 2004

"It's certainly not groundbreaking news that the early victories by the women on 'The Apprentice' were, to a very large extent, dependent on their sex appeal."
How To Get Rich, 2004

"I've been so lucky in terms of that whole world. It is a dangerous world out there — it's scary, like Vietnam. Sort of like the Vietnam era. It is my personal Vietnam. I feel like a great and very brave soldier." — on sleeping with women who could have STDs,
Howard Stern, 2004

> Donald Trump insists that he's always had a great relationship with women. He said, "I believe a woman can be anything she wants to be whether that's Miss Teen USA or Miss Universe."
> **— Conan O'Brien**

"First of all, she's unbelievably short, and I'm a little bit surprised. I think the boob job is terrible. They look like 2 light bulbs coming out of a body. I would say she's an 8."
Howard Stern Show, December 7, 2005

On Carmen Electra

"Nobody cares about the talent [in beauty pageants]. There's only one talent you care about, and that's the look talent. You don't give a shit if a girl can play a violin like the greatest violinist in the world. You want to know what does she look like."
Trump Nation, 2005

"She's really cute, I have to tell you, she's really bouncy, really cute, She's about 5-foot-1. Do you like girls that are 5-foot-1? They come up to you know where."
Howard Stern Show, 2005

On Eva Longoria

"She's very, very short. You know, she goes out with a basketball player, which is interesting, but she's very short."
Howard Stern Show, 2005

On Eva Longoria

"A person who is very flat-chested is very hard to be a 10"
Howard Stern Show, 2005

On Nicolette Sheridan

They were rating the attractiveness of the Desperate Housewives

"Would you go out with Marcia Cross or would you turn gay, Howard?"
Howard Stern Show, 2005

> "Now, if you're a woman and hear Tic Tacs shaking in someone's pocket, it's like hearing the Jaws theme."
> **—Colin Jost**

"My favourite part (of the movie Pulp Fiction) is when Sam has his gun out in the diner and he tells the guy to tell his girlfriend to shut up. Tell that bitch to be cool. Say: Bitch be cool. I love those lines."
TrumpNation: The Art of Being The Donald, 2005

> "Donald Trump owns the Miss USA Pageant, which is great for Republicans since it will streamline their search for a vice-president."
> — **Seth Meyers**

"Well, I'll tell you the funniest is that before a show, I'll go backstage and everyone's getting dressed, and everything else, and you know, no men are anywhere, and I'm allowed to go in because I'm the owner of the pageant and therefore I'm inspecting it," Trump said. "You know, I'm inspecting because I want to make sure that everything is good."
"You know, the dresses. 'Is everyone okay?' You know, they're standing there with no clothes. 'Is everybody okay?' And you see these incredible looking women, and so, I sort of get away with things like that.

Howard Stern Show, April 2005

Howard Stern: Do you think you could now be banging 24-year-olds?

TRUMP: Oh, absolutely.

STERN: Would you do it?

TRUMP: I'd have no problem.

STERN: Do you have an age limit?

TRUMP: No, I have no age — I mean, I have age limit. I don't want to be like Congressman Foley, with, you know, 12-year-olds.
> **The Howard Stern Show, 2006**

**Allegation No. 5
...some were as young as 15.**

1997: Four women who competed in the Miss USA pageant alleged to BuzzFeed News that Trump walked into the dressing room while the girls were changing. Tasha Dixon, who competed as Miss USA Arizona in 2001 said: "He just came strolling right in. There was no second to put a robe on or any sort of clothing or anything. Some girls were topless. Other girls were naked." Some of the contestants in Miss Teen USA were as young as 15. **"Don't worry, ladies, I've seen it all before," Trump allegedly said.**

"Some women are highly aggressive and they want sex, no different from men and sometimes worse."
Trump University Blog, September 17, 2006

"[Angelina Jolie's] been with so many guys she makes me look like a baby... And, I just don't even find her attractive."
Larry King Live, October 9, 2006

> "People look at the Statue of Liberty and they see a proud symbol of our history as a nation of immigrants, a beacon of hope for people around the world. Donald looks at the Statue of Liberty and sees a four. Maybe a five, if she loses the torch and tablet and changes her hair."
>
> **—Hillary Clinton**

"Angelina Jolie is sort of amazing because everyone thinks she's like this great beauty. And I'm not saying she's an unattractive woman, but she's not a beauty, by any stretch of the imagination. I really understand beauty."
CNN, Oct. 9, 2006

**Allegation No. 6
Oh my God, gross...**

1997: Temple Taggart McDowell, a 21-year-old Miss USA contestant, said Donald Trump forcibly kissed her on the mouth during a pageant rehearsal."He kissed me directly on the lips. I thought, 'Oh my God, gross.' she told The New York Times. "He was married to Marla Maples at the time. I think there were a few other girls that he kissed on the mouth. I was like 'Wow, that's inappropriate.'"

"If I were running 'The View', I'd fire Rosie O'Donnell. I mean, I'd look at her right in that fat, ugly face of hers, I'd say 'Rosie, you're fired.'"
Entertainment Tonight, December 21, 2006

"Rosie O'Donnell's disgusting. I mean, both inside and out. You take a look at her, she's a slob ..."
Entertainment Tonight, December 21, 2006

"She called me a snake oil salesman, and, you know, coming from Rosie, that's pretty low, because when you look at her, and when you see the mind, the mind is—is weak. I don't see it. I don't get it. I never understood. How does she even get on television?"
Entertainment Tonight, December 21, 2006)

"Rosie's a person that's very lucky to have her girlfriend. And she better be careful or I'll send one of my friends over to pick up her girlfriend. Why would she stay with Rosie if she had another choice?"
Entertainment Tonight, December. 21, 2006

"I think she's a terrible person. I can look at people and see what they are."
New York Post, December 22, 2006

"Rosie O'Donnell's disgusting both inside and out. You take a look at her, she's a slob. She talks like a truck driver, she doesn't have her facts, she'll say anything that comes to her mind. Her show failed when it was a talk show, the ratings went very, very, very low and very bad, and she got essentially thrown off television. I mean she's basically a disaster."
The Insider, 2006

On fighting Rosie O'Donnell:

"I think it'd be pretty close — if she ever fell in the wrong direction I wouldn't have a chance."
"She was at the wedding and I got extremely angry because she ate almost the entire wedding cake."
Howard Stern Show, 2007

"When Beyonce was thrusting her hips forward in a very suggestive manner [during her Super Bowl Halftime performance], if someone else would have done that it would have been a national scandal"
The Howard Stern Show, 2013

"They'll walk up, and they'll flip their top, and they'll flip their panties."
Howard Stern, 2007

Allegation No. 7
Don't you know who I am?

1998: Karena Virginia, 27, claims Trump grabbed her right arm and groped her breast when she was at the U.S. Open. "'Don't you know who I am, don't you know who I am,' he said," Virginia explained during a press conference with Gloria Allred. "I felt intimidated and I felt powerless."

"Oftentimes when I was sleeping with one of the top women in the world I would say to myself, thinking about me as a boy from Queens, 'Can you believe what I am getting?'"
Think Big: Make it Happen in Business and Life, 2008.

"I think Gloria [Allred] would be very, very impressed with [my penis]."
TMZ Live, April 3, 2012

"26,000 unreported sexual assults [sic] in the military — only 238 convictions. What did these geniuses expect when they put men & women together?"
Twitter, May 7, 2013

**Allegation No. 8
Donald just grabbed my ass**

2003: Mindy McGillivray claims the Donald groped her at Mar-a-Lago: The woman, then 23, told the Palm Beach Post on Wednesday: "All of a sudden I felt a grab, a little nudge. I think it's Ken's camera bag, that was my first instinct. I turn around and there's Donald. He sort of looked away quickly." McGillivray said she recalls telling the photographer, Ken Davidoff, "Donald just grabbed my ass."

"She's gotten a little bit large, I would say this, I don't think you should dress like you weigh 120 pounds."
Showbiz Tonight, 2013

Trump weighs in on Kim Kardashian's pregnancy

"O.K.," I said. "You're basically alone. Your wife is still asleep"—he was then married, but not for much longer, to Marla Maples—"you're in the bathroom shaving and you see yourself in the mirror. What are you thinking?"

From Trump, a look of incomprehension.

Me: "I mean, are you looking at yourself and thinking, 'Wow. I'm Donald Trump?'"
Trump remained baffled.

Me: "O.K., I guess I'm asking, do you consider yourself ideal company?"

At the time, I deemed Trump's reply unprintable. But that was then.

Trump: "You really want to know what I consider ideal company?"

Me: "Yes."

Trump: "A total piece of ass."

Mark Singer, The New Yorker, April 2011

TRUMP: (To Brande Roderick) Excuse me, you dropped to your knees?

BRANDE: Yes,

TRUMP: Must be a pretty picture, you dropping to your knees.
Celebrity Apprentice, 2013

"Love him or hate him, Donald Trump is a man who is certain about what he wants and sets out to get it, no holds barred," Trump said about himself one time. "Women find his power almost as much of a turn-on as his money."
Jeffery Kluger/BoingBoing, September 9, 2014

On behalf of women everywhere, we hate it when men talk about themselves in the third person.

Allegation No. 9
...he thought I was so insignificant that he could do that

2005: Rachel Crooks, who was working at the real-estate company with offices in Trump Tower, told The New York Times that after a handshake, Trump began kissing her on the cheeks and then directly on the mouth. "It was so inappropriate," Crooks said. "I was so upset that he thought I was so insignificant that he could do that."

"Well, absolutely. It's record-setting. In the old days, they'd say she has a bad body" — On whether Kim Kardashian's butt is too big,
Howard Stern Show, 2014.

"I went to a military academy, which was from a different planet; We didn't have women in the academy at that time. Today you have women, which is a whole other story, women in the army and you see what's going on. It's like bedlam."

"It is bedlam. It's something that people aren't talking about but what's going on is bedlam, bringing women in the army."

"Raped and they can't even report it because—So, again, the whole thing is… Look, our country is so…"
Interview with Michael D'Antonio,
The Truth About Trump, 2014

"If Hillary Clinton can't satisfy her husband what makes her think she can satisfy America?"
Twitter, April 16, 2015

> **Allegation No. 10**
> **...and forcing his tongue down my throat.**
>
> **2005:** Reporter Natasha Stoynoff was on the Trump beat for People, when she was invited to Mar-A-Lago to report on Donald and Melania's first wedding anniversary. Stoynoff writes, Trump said he had a "tremendous" room to show her and led her into another room and shut the door. "Within seconds, he was pushing me against the wall, and forcing his tongue down my throat.""You know we're going to have an affair, don't you?" Trump allegedly said after the attack was interrupted by his butler.

"Heidi Klum. Sadly, she's no longer a 10."
New York Times, August 2015

Klum responded by posting a video on Twitter, in which a man wearing a Trump mask ripped a number 10 off of her T-shirt, revealing a 9.99 underneath.

MEGYN KELLY: You've called women you don't like 'fat pigs,' 'dogs,' 'slobs' and 'disgusting animals.'

TRUMP: Only Rosie O'Donnell.
GOP debate, August 2015

"Frankly what I say and oftentimes it's fun, it's kidding, we have a good time,"
GOP debate, August 2015

How he justifies calling women dogs, slobs and pigs.

"You could see there was blood coming out of her eyes. Blood coming out of her wherever."
CNN, August 7, 2015

Donald Trump, insulting Fox News anchor Megyn Kelly over questions she asked during the first Republican primary debate

> "Trump threatening not to show up for next debate if Megyn Kelly is moderating! I bet he's so mad he has 'blood coming out of his wherever.'"
> **—Bette Midler**

"I cherish women. I want to help women. I'm going to be able to do things for women that no other candidate would be able to do ... "
CNN, August 9, 2015

> **Allegation No. 11**
> **What is happening?**
>
> **2006:** A local Finnish newspaper reports that Miss Finland in 2006, Ninni Laaksonen, claims Trump grabbed her on the behind just before she appeared on the Late Show with David Letterman. "Trump stood right next to me and suddenly he squeezed my butt. He really grabbed my butt," she said. "I don't think anybody saw it but I flinched and thought: 'What is happening?'"

"I will be phenomenal to the women. I mean, I want to help women."
CBS' Face the Nation, August. 9, 2015

"I have many women that work for me."
CBS' Face the Nation, August. 9, 2015

"I will be so good to women."
CNN, August. 10, 2015

"@MeghanMcCain was terrible on @TheFive yesterday. Angry and obnoxious, she will never make it on T.V. @FoxNews can do so much better!"

Twitter, September 5, 2015

"Look at that face! Would anyone vote for that? Can you imagine that, the face of our next president I mean, she's a woman, and I'm not s'posedta say bad things, but really, folks, come on. Are we serious?"

Rolling Stone, September 9, 2015

On Carly Fiorina, former CEO of HP

> During that debate, Fiorina took Trump to task for his comments. "I think women all over the country heard very clearly what Mr Trump said," she said, to supportive applause.
>
> Trump, momentarily lost for words, was left awkwardly back-pedalling, and said: "I think she has a very beautiful face."
>
> **The Guardian, November 10, 2015**

"Why does she keep interrupting everybody?"
GOP Debate, November 10, 2015

Singling out Carly Fiorina [the only women] during a debate that saw everyone talking over each other.

"I know where she went – it's disgusting, I don't want to talk about it. No, it's too disgusting. Don't say it, it's disgusting."
GOP Debate, December 19, 2015

Holy Hang-ups! Donald Trump on Hillary Clinton taking a bathroom break during a Democratic presidential debate

---

Allegation No. 12
"thrusting his genitals"

2007: Former Apprentice contestant Summer Zervos accused Trump of groping her and trying to have sex with during a job interview. Zervos who had come to his golf course in Palos Verdes, California to discuss a job opportunity, said Trump kissed her forcibly on the lips several times and groped her. A second time, Trump allegedly walked her into a bedroom and began "thrusting his genitals" at her before she told him to stop.

"Listen to this. We won with everything. We won with women. I love the women. We won with women." (Cheers and applause)
Atlanta, February 22, 2016

"Lyin' Ted Cruz just used a picture of Melania from a G.Q. shoot in his ad. Be careful, Lyin' Ted, or I will spill the beans on your wife!"
Twitter, March 22, 2016

> Pic of your wife not from us. Donald, if you try to attack Heidi, you're more of a coward than I thought. #classless— Ted Cruz (@tedcruz)
> ### Twitter, March 23, 2016

Allegation No. 13
Trump took Tic Tacs

2010: CNN anchor Erin Burnett relays a story from a friend about Trump attempting an unprompted kiss. "Trump took Tic Tacs, suggested I take them also. He then leaned in, catching me off guard, and kissed me almost on lips. I was really freaked out," Burnett quoted her friend as saying. Afterward, the friend said Trump told her how "special I am" and asked her to call him.

"Given his draconian comment, sending women back to back alleys, I had to ask: When he was a swinging bachelor in Manhattan, was he ever involved with anyone who had an abortion?"

'Such an interesting question,' he said. 'So what's your next question?'"

**NYT, Maureen Dowd
April 2, 2016**

TRUMP ON ABORTION

"I'm very pro-choice," Trump says. "I hate the concept of abortion. I hate it. I hate everything it stands for. I cringe when I listen to people debating the subject. But you still — I just believe in choice."

Russert clarifies his original point: Would you ban partial-birth abortion?

"No," Trump replies.
NBC, Tim Russert, October 24, 1999

"I am pro-life. Against gun control…
CPAC Conference, February 10, 2011

130

In an interview with MSNBC's Savannah Guthrie, Trump was asked if he believes there's a right to privacy in the Constitution.

The question is an important one in the abortion debate. Pro-lifers say there absolutely is not a Constitutional right to privacy, which means Roe is a travesty and abortion should once again be permitted to be outlawed in the states that choose to do so. Pro-choicers strenuously disagree, stating that the right to privacy is guaranteed and is extended to a woman's choice to have an abortion or not, the central basis of Roe.

Trump ...appeared to have no understanding of the connection ...

"I guess there is, I guess there is," Trump said when Guthrie asked if there's a Constitutional right to privacy. "And why, just out of curiosity, why do you ask that question?"

Guthrie informed him of the connection to abortion, but Trump seemed surprised that the two went together:

"Well, that's a pretty strange way of getting to pro-life. I mean, it's a very unique way of asking about pro-life. What does that have to do with privacy? How are you equating pro-life with privacy?"

Talking Points Memo, DC, April 19, 2011

CNN Interview With Jake Tapper

TAPPER: Let me ask you about a few social issues because they haven't been issues you have been talking about for several years. I know you're opposed to abortion.

TRUMP: Right. I'm pro-choice.

TAPPER: You're pro-choice or pro-life?

TRUMP: I'm pro-life. I'm sorry.
June 28, 2015

March 30, 2016, 2:30 p.m.

An interview with [Chris] Matthews is taped, where Trump asserts that women who receive abortions once the procedure is illegal will face punishment. The men involved will not. News of the comments quickly leaks.

March 30, 2016, 3:30 p.m.

Before the MSNBC town hall even airs, a spokesperson for Trump releases a statement changing what he told Matthews.

"The issue is unclear and should be put back into the States for determination. Like Ronald Reagan, I am pro-life

with exceptions, which I have outlined numerous times. — Donald J Trump"
The Washington Post

March 30, 2016, 5 p.m.

An hour later, Trump released a "statement regarding abortion." It's different than his answer to Chris Matthews, which is about to air:

"If Congress were to pass legislation making abortion illegal and the federal courts upheld this legislation, or any state were permitted to ban abortion under state and federal law," the statement says, "the doctor or any other person performing this illegal act upon a woman would be held legally responsible, not the woman."

Then the interview with Chris Mathews airs...

"There has to be some form of punishment...you go back to a position like they had where they would perhaps go to illegal places, but we have to ban it."
MSNBC Town Hall, March 30, 2016

Asked about abortion again the next day, Trump's position changed yet again.

"The laws are set now on abortion and that's the way they're going to remain until they're changed, I would've preferred states' rights. I think it would've been better if it were up to the states. But right now, the laws are set.... At this moment, the laws are set. And I think we have to leave it that way."
     Face the Nation, April 1, 2016

Hope Hicks from the Trump Campaign released another statement to CBS, that same day, clarifying (walking back) his statement, once again:

"Mr. Trump gave an accurate account of the law as it is today and made clear it must stay that way now --until he is President," Hicks said. "Then he will change the law through his judicial appointments and allow the states to protect the unborn. There is nothing new or different here."

"I think the only card she has is the women's card. She has got nothing else going. Frankly, if Hillary Clinton were a man, I don't think she would get 5% of the vote. And the beautiful thing is women don't like her, ok?"
    Victory Press Conference,
    New York, April 26, 2016

"Number one, I have great respect for women. I was the one that really broke the glass ceiling on behalf of women, more than anybody in the construction industry. My relationship, I think, is going to end up being very good with women."
    O'Reilly Factor, June 3, 2016

Allegation No. 14
He continually grabbed my ass

2013: Cassandra Searles, a former Miss Washington who participated in the Miss USA pageant, posted the following on Facebook, "he continually grabbed my ass and invited me to his hotel room," reported by Seattle's KING-TV.

"I would say with women, if they qualify [to join the military] — and I have to say there are very few that qualify from a certain standpoint,"
    Fox News, July 13, 2016

"Well, obviously it's great outer beauty. I mean, we could say politically correct that look doesn't matter, but the look obviously matters. Like you wouldn't have your job if you weren't beautiful."
To a female reporter, Video Clip from Last Week Tonight, 2016

"She was the worst we ever had. The worst. The absolute worst. She was impossible... She was the winner, and she gained a massive amount of weight, and it was a real problem. We had a real problem."
Fox & Friends, September 27, 2016

Trump's efforts to explain why he referred to Miss Universe 1996, Alicia Machado as "Miss Piggy."

**Allegation No. 15
What do you want? How much?**

2006: Jessica Drake, an adult film star met Trump at a charity gold tournament...."In the penthouse suite, I met Donald again," Drake continued. "When we entered the room, he grabbed each of us tightly in a hug and kissed each one of us without asking permission. He was wearing pajamas. A bodyguard was also present.

"These are stories that are made up, these are total fiction. You'll find out that, in the years to come, these women that stood up, it was all fiction. They were made up. I don't know these women, it's not my thing to do what they say. You know I don't do that."

"I don't grab them, as they say, on the arm; One said, 'He grabbed me on the arm.' And she's a porn star. You know, this one that came out recently, 'He grabbed me and he grabbed me on the arm.' Oh, I'm sure she's never been grabbed before."
WGIR, October 24, 2016

SNYDER: You have two beautiful daughters past their teenage years; Can you understand the concern from parents of younger girls that some of your comments could be hurtful to girls struggling with body image and the pressure to be model-perfect?

TRUMP: Sure I do. And you know, a lot of this is done in the entertainment business. I'm being interviewed for *Apprentice* long before I ever thought in terms of running for office.

But a lot of that was done for the purpose of entertainment. I can tell you this: There is nobody — nobody — that has more respect for women than I do.
KSNV Las Vegas, October 5, 2016

TRUMP
Birther-in-Chief

"A new poll shows that one of the major parties in this country – I won't tell you which one – is a majority birther party. That's right, more than half of Republicans now think Obama was born in Kenya. They literally do not know where babies come from."

—**Bill Maher**

"Everybody who gives even a hint of being a birther... even a little bit of a hint... they label them as an idiot... Let me tell you, I'm a really smart guy. The reason I have a little doubt -- just a little -- is because he grew up, and nobody knew him. If ever I got the nomination, if I ever decide to run, you may go back and interview people from my kindergarten. They'll remember me. Nobody ever comes forward. Nobody knows who he is until later in his life. It's very strange. The whole thing is very strange."

**Good Morning America,
March 17, 2011**

"I've seen people take a $100 bill and make a $1,000,000 bill,"(...) "There's something on that birth certificate that [Obama] doesn't like. Why doesn't he show his birth certificate? There's something on that birth certificate that he doesn't like."

The View March 23, 2011

Whoopi Goldberg said it was "the biggest pile of dog mess I've heard in ages."

"He's spent millions of dollars trying to get away from this issue. Millions of dollars in legal fees trying to get away from this issue. And I'll tell you what, I brought it up, just routinely, and all of a sudden a lot of facts are emerging and I'm starting to wonder myself whether or not he was born in this country."
- **Fox and Friends March 28, 2011**

FOX NEWS — THE O'REILLY FACTOR

O'REILLY: Now, when you were on "The View" and they didn't walk out, which they should have because they walked out on me and they should have stayed. You were way, way worse than I was on "The View." You were hammering the birth certificate.

Now, we very early on did an investigation about Barack Obama's birth certificate. What "The Factor" found out was there were two announcements the week he was born in both Honolulu newspapers saying that he was born, OK. That is impossible -- that is impossible to make happen if he had not been born in the hospital. So therefore, I just put it to bed. I said he was born in Honolulu. The two newspapers documented it. His mother was a hippy. His father was a guy from Kenya who split. There couldn't have been a sophisticated -- what is he, Baby Jesus? -- there was a sophisticated conspiracy to smuggle this baby back into the country? So I just dismissed it. But you made a big deal of it.

TRUMP: Bill, I grew up with Wall Street geniuses. What they do in terms of fraud and how they change documents and I will tell you something. If you notice those dates were three days later. Here is what I ask people. Who puts announcements? Here are two poor people, a man and a woman with no money, they have a baby. There's announcements in the newspaper?

O'REILLY: The grandparents did it.

TRUMP: Excuse me. The grandparents. Nelson Rockefeller doesn't put announcements.

O'REILLY: Sure, there are birth announcements all the time.

TRUMP: I have never seen one.

O'REILLY: Really? They are common.

TRUMP: I've never seen one.

O'REILLY: But why is this important to you?

TRUMP: Because if you are going to be president of the United States you have to be born in this country. And there is a doubt as to whether or not he was born…

O'REILLY: Oh come on. Do you really feel this about him?

TRUMP: You know, I started off by saying -- and I always do and I did on the "The View." I'm a very smart guy. I went to the best college. I had good marks. I was a very smart guy, good student and all that stuff. Because what they do to the birthers, which is a term I hate because a lot of these birthers are just really quality people that just want the truth. What they do to the birthers is unbelievable to a point where people are afraid to talk about this subject. They are afraid to confront you or anybody about this subject.

O'REILLY: Do you think it's an important subject?

TRUMP: Listen, I have a birth certificate. I have my birth certificate. And in fact, they said the one I gave yesterday wasn't good enough. So I actually got the one from the Health Department, which is the perfect one. Because they were saying the one I gave yesterday wasn't good enough, so I got the other. People have birth certificates. He doesn't have a birth certificate. He may have one but there's something on that, maybe religion, maybe it says he is a Muslim. I don't know. Maybe he doesn't want that. Or he may not have one. But I will tell you this. If he wasn't born in this country, it's one of the great scams of all time.

**Fox News, O'Reilly Factor,
March 30, 2011**

"I have a birth certificate. People have birth certificates. He doesn't have a birth certificate. He may have one but there is something on that birth certificate -- maybe religion, maybe it says he's a Muslim, I don't know. Maybe he doesn't want that. Or, he may not have one."
The Laura Ingraham Show
March 30, 2011

"He doesn't have a birth certificate, or if he does, there's something on that certificate that is very bad for him. Now, somebody told me -- and I have no idea if this is bad for him or not, but perhaps it would be -- that where it says 'religion,' it might have 'Muslim.' And if you're a Muslim, you don't change your religion, by the way."
The Laura Ingram Show
March 30, 2011

NBC'S THE TODAY SHOW WITH MEREDITH VIERA

VIERA: You have spent a lot of time talking about President Obama's birth certificate, or lack thereof, you don't seem convinced that he has one..

TRUMP: I'm not convinced that he has one. I've had very smart people tell me, "Donald....(list various issues...), stay off...

VIERA: Stay off the birth certificate issue. Why don't you?

TRUMP: Because, you know why?, because three weeks ago when I started, I thought he was probably born in this country, and I really have a much bigger doubt than I had before...

VIERA: Based on what?

TRUMP: And you know what? His grandmother in Kenya says he was born in Kenya and she was there and witnessed the birth, okay? He doesn't have a birth certificate, or he hasn't shown it. He has a certificate of live birth is something that's easy to get. When you want a birth certificate it's very hard to get.
(Crosstalk)

VIERA: It's the equivalent. In the State of Hawaii, they say that they have seen this document and he was born in the United States....

TRUMP: (Talking Over) It's not the equivalent.

VIERA: It's good enough for them. Scholars have looked....

TRUMP: A birth certificate is not even close. A certificate of live birth is not even signed by anybody. I saw his. I read it very carefully, doesn't have a serial number, doesn't have a signature…

VIERA: Do you believe he's lying? (crosstalk)

TRUMP: I'm starting to believe he was not born here…

VIERA: Do you believe he is lying? (crosstalk) Do You believe he's lying Donald, come on, just answer

TRUMP: Meredith! He spent two million dollars in legal fees trying to get away from this issue. If he weren't lying why wouldn't he just solve it?..and I would, and I wish he would because if he doesn't, it's one of the greatest scams in the history of politics and in the history period. You are not allowed to be a president if you were not born in this country and he may not be born in this country and I'll tell you what, three weeks ago I thought he was born in this country. Right now I have some real doubts. I have people who have been studying it, and they can't believe what they are finding…

VIERA: You have people now (crosstalk)

TRUMP: Absolutely..

VIERA: down there searching, I mean in Hawaii…

TRUMP: And they cannot believe what they are finding. I would like to have him show his birth certificate…and can I be honest with you…I hope he can; because if he can't, if he can't, if he wasn't born in this country, and that's a real possibility, I'm not saying it happened, I'm saying it's a REAL possibility, much greater than I thought two or three weeks ago — then he has pulled one of the greatest cons in the history of politics.
  Today Show, April 7, 2011

"He grew up and nobody knew him. You know? When you interview people, if ever I got the nomination, if I ever decide to run, you may go back and interview people from my kindergarten. They'll remember me. Nobody ever comes forward. Nobody knows who he his until later in his life. It's very strange. The whole thing is very strange."
  Good Morning America, 2011

"His grandmother in Kenya said, 'Oh, no, he was born in Kenya and I was there and I witnessed the birth.' She's on tape. I think that tape's going to be produced fairly soon. Somebody is coming out with a book in two weeks, it will be very interesting."
  MSNBC's Morning Joe
  April 7, 2011

"We've had every official in Hawaii, Democrat and Republican, every news outlet that has investigated this confirm that, yes, in fact, I was born in Hawaii August 4th, 1961, in Kapiolani Hospital," he said. "We've posted the certification that is given by the state of Hawaii on the Internet for everybody to see. People have provided affidavits that they, in fact, have seen this birth certificate. And yet this thing just keeps on going."

**—President Barack Obama,
Releasing his birth certificate
April 27, 2011**

"I've been told very recently, Anderson, that the birth certificate is missing. I've been told that it's not there or it doesn't exist. And if that's the case, it's a big problem."

**To CNN's Anderson Cooper:
April 25, 2011**

"We're looking into it very, very strongly. At a certain point in time I'll be revealing some interesting things," ... You'll be very surprised,"

**CNN's American Morning.
April 27, 2011**

The attempt to otherize Obama began in 2004, after he delivered the keynote address at the Democratic convention in Boston. "Obama is a Muslim who has concealed his religion" was the initial claim pushed out in a press release written by serial litigant and failed candidate Andy Martin—who once ran for Congress vowing to "Exterminate Jew Power in America." The claim was then aggregated by conservative media.

**Olivia Nuzzi, The Daily Beast
September 16, 2016**

President Obama Jokes About Trump at the White House Correspondents' Dinner 2011

My FELLOW Americans, Mahalo! ….As some of you heard, the State of Hawaii released my OFFICIAL long form birth certificate. Hopefully this puts all doubts to rest, but just in case there are any lingering questions, tonight, I'm prepared to go a step further. Tonight, for the first time, I am releasing my official birth video …(plays short clip from The Lion King)…I, uh, wanna make clear to the Fox News table, that was a joke. That was not my real birth video. That was a children's cartoon. Call Disney if you don't believe me, they have the original long-form version……(generally KILLS IT for 5 minutes of unrelated humour)….

Michelle Bachman is here. I understand she is thinking of running for president; which is weird because I understand she was born in Canada. — Yes, Michelle, this is how it starts. Donald Trump! He's here tonight. Now, I know he's taken some flak lately, but no one is happier, no one is prouder to put this birth certificate matter to rest than the Donald, and that's because he can finally get back to focusing on the issue that matter, like did we fake the moon landing, what really happened in Roswell and where are Biggie and Tupac?

All kidding aside, obviously we all know about your credentials and breadth of experience, (big laugh rises from crowd) For example, no…uhmmm… seriously…recently, in an episode of Celebrity Apprentice, at the steakhouse, the men's cooking team did not impress the judges from Omaha Steaks; and there was a lot of blame to go around, but you Mr. Trump recognized that the real problem was a lack of leadership — so, ultimately, you didn't blame Lil' Jon or Meatloaf; You fired Gary Busey…and these are the kind of decisions that would keep me up at night.

April 30, 2011

""I am really honored frankly to have played such a big role in hopefully, hopefully, getting rid of this issue," he said. "We have to look at it, we have to see is it real, is it proper, what's on it, but I hope it checks out beautifully. I am really proud, I am really honored. It is rather amazing that all the sudden it materializes, but I hope it's the right deal. I'm really proud that I was able to bring this to a point."

New Hampshire, April 27, 2011

> "President Obama released his long-form birth certificate, proving once and for all he was born in this country. But you know, it never ends. Now Republican leaders are saying they want to see the placenta."
>
> **–Jay Leno**

"A lot of people do not think it was an authentic certificate. ... Many people do not think it was authentic. His mother was not in the hospital. There are many other things that came out. And frankly if you would report it accurately I think you'd probably get better ratings than you're getting."

To CNN's Wolf Blitzer, May 29, 2012

"Everybody's entitled to your opinion. You know my opinion and you know his opinion and that's fine. We're entitled - as he said yesterday in the airplane - we're all entitled to our opinions and he's entitled to have his opinion. I don't happen to share that opinion, it's wonderful."
To CNN's Wolf Blitzer, May 29, 2012

Donald entitles himself to his own facts — calls Obama's birth certificate his "opinion"

Blitzer presents Trump with the newspaper announcements of Obama's birth from 1961

TRUMP: Can you stop defending Obama?

BLITZER: Donald, you're beginning to sound a little ridiculous, I have to tell you.

TRUMP: You are, Wolf! Let me tell you something, I think YOU sound ridiculous!
CNN, May 29, 2012

"He didn't know he was running for president, so he told the truth. The literary agent wrote down what he said ... He said he was born in Kenya and raised in Indonesia ... Now they're saying it was a mistake. Just like his Kenyan grandmother said he was born in

153

Kenya, and she pointed down the road to the hospital, and after people started screaming at her, she said, 'Oh, I mean Hawaii.' Give me a break."
> **The Daily Beast with Lloyd Grove**
> **May 24, 2012**

Dr. Alvin Onaka, the Hawaii state registrar who handled queries about Mr. Obama, said recently through a spokeswoman that he had no evidence or recollection of Mr. Trump or any of his representatives ever requesting the records from the Hawaii State Department of Health.

But not only was Trump peddling racist garbage, he appears to have also been lying about his own efforts. While he told a national television audience that he'd "absolutely" dispatched investigators to Hawaii, and those investigators had turned up extraordinary evidence, the Times' latest reporting suggests Trump made up the whole thing: the investigators and the findings existed solely in Trump's mind.

I can appreciate why this seems like old news – even he doesn't push this particular nonsense anymore – but the revelation from the weekend nevertheless sheds new light on the 2016 candidate. Trump's willingness to peddle a racist conspiracy theory told us something important about his character, but his willingness to lie to his own supporters about his efforts adds insult to injury.
> **Steve Benen, MSNBC, July 5, 201**

"An 'extremely credible source' and told me that @BarackObama's birth certificate is a fraud"
Twitter, August 6, 2012

"These people could have personally witnessed Obama being born out of an apple pie, in the middle of a Kansas wheat field, while Toby Keith sang the National Anthem — and they'd still think he was a Kenyan Muslim."

–Jimmy Kimmel

CNN'S ON THE RECORD WITH GRETA VAN SUSTEREN:

VAN SUSTEREN: Well, Donald, you've done it again! You've gotten everybody's attention. So tell me exactly what is the challenge that you have posed to the president of the United States?

TRUMP: (...BLAH...BLAH...BLAH...)

VAN SUSTEREN: What do you want? What are you looking for that you think is worth $5 million to charity? You haven't made an offer on the table for Governor Romney, so I figure you must be thinking there is something that is valuable?

TRUMP: No, I think that people want to see. You have no idea. I get millions and millions of hits on just please stay with this. I walk down the street, people love me over it. I went to North Carolina, made a speech. The most important thing was the issue of location, place of birth, et cetera. I went to Liberty University, made a speech, incredible school. I mean, they loved this —

VAN SUSTEREN: What —

TRUMP: Greta, this is a very important issue. This is a very important issue.

VAN SUSTEREN: Are you not satisfied with the presentation of the documents of his birth? Are we going back to that?

TRUMP: Well, I am not sure about it. Other people are not sure. All have you to do is pick up the newspapers and you will see. Many people have serious questions about what he presented. There were many, many people. So I am —

VAN SUSTEREN: Excuse me —

(CROSSTALK)

VAN SUSTEREN: There are two questions. I thought the birth issue was established that you were satisfied. You got the president to produce his long-firm birth certificate.

TRUMP: I did. And Greta, nobody else was able to do that.

VAN SUSTEREN: Right. I thought that you were satisfied. He met the constitutional requirements. Now you want these other records. I am trying to figure out why. Is it like you want to see what kind of student he was —

TRUMP: Greta, why are you speaking for me? I never said I was satisfied. I never told you that I was satisfied?

VAN SUSTEREN: Oh, I didn't know that.

TRUMP: Excuse me, who is satisfied? Pick up the newspapers, there are many, many people, tremendous numbers of people that are not satisfied. There is tremendous skepticism as to what he presented. Unbelievable skepticism —

VAN SUSTEREN: I stand corrected. I apologize. I apologize for getting it wrong. I am satisfied. I made a mistake —

TRUMP: Are you satisfied?

VAN SUSTEREN: Yes.

TRUMP: I am very surprised at you. I am very surprised at you. I don't know how you can be satisfied. But if you are satisfied, you are less skeptical than me.

I grew up in the real estate business in New York, Greta. I have seen everything.

VAN SUSTEREN: All right, let me ask you a question, in these college records, is there something else that you are looking for besides the issue about birth?

TRUMP: Greta, let's see what it says! You are talking about a tremendous amount of money for charity. Let's see what it says. Who knows! I mean, if you ask me, what do we know? You don't know anything, Greta. For you to say -- I really am surprised at you. You don't know anything. For you to say that you are satisfied is really shocking to me, to be honest with you. When you ask me, what do you think? Let's find out. I can't tell what you I think because I don't know. I haven't seen the papers —

CNN's On the Record, October 24, 2012

"Was it a birth certificate? You tell me. Some people say that was not his birth certificate. Maybe it was, maybe it wasn't. I'm saying I don't know. Nobody knows."

ABC News , August 2013

> "I will show you President Obama's birth certificate when you show me Sarah Palin's high school diploma."
>
> —Bill Maher

When I was 18, people called me Donald Trump. When he was 18, @BarackObama was Barry Soweto. Weird.
Twitter, March 12, 2012

Debunked by Snopes: Rumour based on an altered student ID card from 1998. When Obama attended Columbia in 1981, that digital ID system hadn't been introduced yet.

> "That's right: Donald Trump came out as a birther, which is Republican for 'I'm running for president!'"
> **—Lewis Black**

"How amazing, the State Health Director who verified copies of Obama's 'birth certificate' died in plane crash today. All others lived"
Twitter, December 12, 2013

"Amazing?"...how about "tragic?"

"There are three things that could happen. And one of them did happen. He was perhaps born in Kenya. Very simple, OK? He was perhaps born in this country. But said he was born in Kenya because if you say you were born in Kenya, you got aid and you got into colleges. People were doing that. So perhaps he was born in this country, and that has a very big chance. Or, you know, who knows?"

National Press Club, May 27, 2014

"Donald Trump was still saying Obama's birth certificate could be fake last year. And I'm not sure the guy who holds fake press conferences, has a fake university, a fake foundation, fake hair, and a fake tan should be the one in charge of deciding what's real."

—Seth Meyers

IRELAND'S TV3
COLETTE FITZPATRICK

FITZPATRICK: You questioned his citizenship during his campaign, and you said afterwards if he produced that long-form birth certificate, you'd produce your tax returns. But you didn't do it, did you?

TRUMP: Well, I don't know — did he do it? If I decide to run for office I'll produce my tax returns. Absolutely. I would love to do that. I did produce a financial statement even though I wasn't even running. I did produce a financial statement and it was shocking to

some because it was so much higher than people thought possible.

(Trump has not released his tax returns)

The president should come clean. He should have come clean over the years. If you remember the very famous story where I offered him $5 million if he showed some basic records and he never took me up on it. And that would be for charity. So charities would have benefited and it would have been a great thing.

FITZPATRICK: But he is a citizen and he produced that long form birth certificate.

TRUMP: Well, a lot of people don't agree with you and a lot of people feel it wasn't a proper certificate.

Ireland TV3's Colette Fitzpatrick
May 2014

MEET THE PRESS

CHUCK TODD: Do you believe President Obama is a citizen who was born in the United States?

DONALD TRUMP: Well, I don't like talking about it

anymore. Because honestly I have my own feelings. I think he should have taken the $5 million. I don't know why he spent $4 million in legal fees to keep his records, you know, away. Nobody's seen his records. I don't know. Maybe--

CHUCK TODD: We're talking about the birth certificate.

DONALD TRUMP: Maybe the hackers. Maybe the hackers have his records. No, I mean, his college records. I mean, he spent $4 million in legal fees to make sure that nobody ever saw--

CHUCK TODD: Well, if you want him to release his--

DONALD TRUMP: So I'll tell you what--

TODD: --would you release all of yours--

TRUMP: But here's what I'll do.

TODD: Would you release all your...

TRUMP: Here's what I'll do--

TODD: ...college transcripts...

TRUMP: I'm proud of my records. But he has to do it. If he does it, I'll do it
                Meet the Press, August 16, 2015

THE LATE SHOW WITH STEPHEN COLBERT

COLBERT: I'm going to throw you a big fat meatball for you to hit out of the park right now; This is the last time you'll ever have to address this question if you hit the ball.

TRUMP: I want to hear this one.

COLBERT: Barack Obama, born in the United States?

(Trump hesitates…)

COLBERT: Meatball…It's a meatball, it's hanging out there…(mimicking a batter's swing) Right there — c'mon.

TRUMP: I don't talk about that anymore.

COLBERT: You don't talk about it?

Trump starts to say that he would rather talk about jobs and veterans, but Colbert cuts him off.

COLBERT: The meatball is now being dragged down subway steps by a rat. You missed the meatball.

The Late Show With Stephen Colbert
September 22, 2015

ABC NEWS WITH JONATHON KARL

KARL: You said a lot of things over the years that people say just make you not serious. One of the big things is on the birth certificate –

TRUMP: Why does that make me not serious? I think that resonated with a lot of people.

KARL: But you don't still question that he was born in the United States, do you?

TRUMP: I have no idea.

KARL: Even at this point?

TRUMP: Well I don't know. Was it a birth certificate? You tell me. Some people say that was not his birth certificate. Maybe it was, maybe it wasn't. I'm saying I don't know. Nobody knows. And you don't know either, Jonathan. You're a smart guy. You don't know either.

KARL: I'm pretty convinced he was born –

TRUMP: Pretty! Ah, pretty, pretty! You said pretty!

KARL: I'm convinced, I'm totally –

TRUMP: No no you said pretty –

KARL: -- totally without question that he was born in the United States.

TRUMP: Excuse me, Jonathan, you said you were pretty convinced. Okay? So let's just see what happens over time. But it's not my issue, Jonathan.

KARL: Okay let me ask you something else –

TRUMP: My issue right now is much different, wait a minute. My issue is economic. Our country is being ripped apart by China and many other countries. That's my issue.

KARL: But isn't it going to be harder for people to take you seriously on those issues if you don't acknowledge that you went overboard on this whole birther stuff?

TRUMP: Well, I don't think I went overboard. Actually, I think it made me very popular, if you want to know the truth, OK? So I do think I know what I'm doing.

KARL: But on this issue, people think that you were just out to lunch.

TRUMP: Well you just said you were pretty sure. And if you're pretty sure, that's not acceptable. Because you can't be pretty sure, you have to be 100 percent.

KARL: I'm sure, I'm 100 percent sure, for the record.

TRUMP: I don't think you are.

KARL: Well let me ask you this. Ted Cruz, born in Canada. Is he eligible to be president of the United States?

TRUMP: Well if he was born in Canada, perhaps not. I'm not sure where he was born.

KARL: Oh he was definitely born in Canada.

TRUMP: Okay well then you'll have to ask him that question. But perhaps not.

KARL: Ted Cruz's mother was an American citizen. He's an American.

TRUMP: Look that will be ironed out. I don't know the circumstances. I heard, somebody told me, that he was born in Canada. That's really his thing.

ABC News with Jonathon Karl
September 7, 2016

"The state of Hawaii passed a new law allowing the state government to ignore requests for President Obama's birth certificate from the 'Birthers.' From now on, every future president should be required to be born on camera and in front of a national landmark."

–Jimmy Kimmel

O'REILLY: Do you think your birther position has hurt you among African-Americans?

TRUMP: I have no idea. I don't talk about it anymore, Bill. Because, you know, I just don't bother talking about it.
**Fox News, The O'Reilly Factor
September 6, 2016**

"President Barack Obama was born in the United States," *Trump said brusquely at the end of a campaign event in his new Washington hotel.* **"Period."**

About 12 hours earlier, senior adviser Jason Miller said in a statement Trump had compelled Obama to release his birth certificate in 2011 to dispel questions about the fact he was born in Hawaii in 1961.
— CNN Politics

"Mr. Trump believes that President Obama was born in the United States," the campaign conceded, a gesture meant to end questions -- which have bubbled up again in the past weeks -- surrounding Republican nominee's role in advancing a fiction meant to delegitimize the first African-American commander in chief. — **CNN Politics**

"Trump himself, however, had not until Friday publicly said he believes Obama was born in the US. And asked recently about his role in promoting the racially charged smear, Trump went uncharacteristically mum."
— **CNN Politics**

"I don't talk about it because if I talk about that, your whole thing will be about that," he told reporters last week. "So I don't talk about it."
    To Reporters, September 15, 2016

Note: On April 27, 2011, President Obama **made public** his long form birth certificate. The Trump campaign in his statement portrayed this as the event that resolved the situation.

"Having successfully obtained President Obama's birth certificate when others could not, Mr. Trump believes that President Obama was born in the United States," Miller said.

But, it wasn't over yet....not in Trump's mind. He continued to stoke the fire...

"Who knows about Obama? ... Who knows, who knows? Who cares right now?... I have my own theory on Obama. Someday I will write a book, I will do another book, and it will do very successfully."
To CNN's Wolf Blitzer, January 6, 2016

"Who is satisfied? All you have to do is pick up the newspapers and there are many, many people, tremendous numbers of people that are not satisfied. There's tremendous skepticism as to what he presented. "
CNN, September 9, 2016

"I'll answer that question at the right time. I just don't want to answer it yet ... I don't talk about it anymore. The reason I don't is because then everyone is going to be talking about it as opposed to jobs, the military, the vets, security."
The Washington Post, September 15, 2016

Oh my God, Barack Obama's running the old Kenyan Prince birth announcement scam.

Here's how it goes: you want to destroy America from the inside but you can't because you're a foreigner. So first, you gotta find yourself a good ol' American to reproduce for you.
Then, you have that child on foreign soil, while simultaneously placing the birth announcement of that child in one of our "fringe" state's local newspapers, your Hawaiis, your Alaskas, your Pennsylvanias.
Alright, then, kidding. And then, hold on, you wait until this baby is a middle-aged man. Now the trap is set.
You just sit back and let that child go out and win the election for President of the United States.

Now here's where the scam gets tricky; they can't just win the popular vote. He or she must have a strategy to win the electoral vote; that's what trips up most drifters. But, if you pull it off, you and your puppet child can sit back and destroy the fabric of the country you both hate so much.

It's almost too easy."

—Jon Stewart

TRUMP
RACIST-IN-CHIEF

"No one's more for the Indians than Donald Trump."

So, I suspect that I am about to tell you something you already know…

Trump's ideas are awful. The man embellishes his fifth grade-level rhetoric like a drag queen with her first Bedazzler….but, (and this drives me bonkers) he utilizes empty adjectives in his speech…almost exclusively — as if he can't think of something genuine to say…Everything is "beautiful," fantastic," YYYUUGE," and "tremendous." He has a rare copy of Webster's Four Word Thesaurus. Everyone has "great spirit" — I picture a team of cheerleaders with pom-poms when he says this — and everything bad is "terrible."

His use of the definite article "the" groups entire races of human beings into undifferentiated masses (who all love him apparently.) In Trump's mind, if you have dark skin, you are one of "the Blacks" and you share common characteristics and life experiences…you live in poverty, you go to a shit school, you kill white people and you are voting for him. And if you, perhaps, went to Columbia and were elected president, then he will offer up $5mil to see your transcripts because he is sure you didn't make it on merit.

Like any good bigot, Trump responds to accusations of bigotry by loudly protesting that he actually loves the group in question. All of the individual human beings that make up the group are essentially one great whole. [I keep seeing Captain Picard when he was wired into the Borg here]

So, while he professes his love of taco bowls and The Hispanics, and touts his great relationship with The Blacks, and certainly between The Muslims and The Gays telling him how fantastic and beautiful, and right he is about everything… Trump thinks he is being complimentary when he sets a group or race apart. Why, "you people" don't seem to know how lucky you are to have the Trump sun shine down on you. That man loves YOU! YOU have "a great spirit" and I have it on his authority that YOUSE are all FANTASTIC!

We are not born hating each other and — even when we don't hate each other — we still aren't born dividing each other into Usses and Thems. Racism is a learned condition, like algebra or salsa dancing. Trump's father was arrested for assaulting two police officers at a Klan rally in NYC in 1927. I don't know for sure, but I doubt that he was there protesting the hate group.

Whether he knows it or not, when Trump empties his head through his mouth, and without thinking, he gives us a glimpse at the beating heart of a real, live racist.

In 1973, the Department of Justice filed charges against the Trump Management Organization for racial discrimination. The case alleged that the Trump Management Corporation had discriminated against blacks who wished to rent apartments in Brooklyn, Queens and Staten Island. The government charged the corporation with quoting different rental terms and conditions to blacks and whites and lying to blacks that apartments were not available. The Feds had a former Trump employee who testified that the organization used to code applications with a "C" for coloured and would steer those renters towards different buildings in the complex that were mostly ethnic.

Huffington Post, April 29, 2011

Two years later, Trump Management settled the case, promising not to discriminate against blacks, Puerto Ricans and other minorities. As part of the agreement, Trump was required to send its list of vacancies in its 15,000 apartments to a civil-rights group, giving them first priority in providing applicants for certain apartments, according to a contemporaneous New York Times account. Trump, who emphasized that the agreement was not an admission of guilt, later crowed that he was satisfied because it did not require them to "accept persons on welfare as tenants unless as qualified as any other tenant."

But the company didn't sufficiently fulfill its promise, because three years later, the Justice Department charged Trump Management with continuing to discriminate against blacks through such tactics as telling them that apartments were not available.

Huffington Post, April 29, 2011

"I have tremendous respect for the Japanese people, I mean, you can respect somebody that's beating the hell out of you."

The Oprah Winfrey Show, 1988

"A well-educated black has a tremendous advantage over a well-educated white in terms of the job market. ... [I]f I were starting off today, I would love to be a well-educated black, because I believe they do have an actual advantage."
NBC News, September 1989

"Who the fuck knows? I mean, really, who knows how much the Japs will pay for Manhattan property these days?"
TIME, January 1989

"The only guys I want counting my money are short guys that wear yarmulkes all day."
USA Today, May 20, 1991

"And isn't it funny. I've got black accountants at Trump Castle and Trump Plaza. Black guys counting my money! I hate it,"
Quoted by John O'Donnell, former President of Trump Castle and Trump Plaza in his 1991 book TRUMPED!

Also from O'Donnell:

"I think the guy is lazy," Trump said of a black employee, "And it's probably not his fault because laziness is a trait in blacks. It really is, I believe that. It's not anything they can control."

> "The stuff O'Donnell wrote about me is probably true"
> **Playboy, 1999**

> "When Donald and Ivana came to the casino, the bosses would order all the black people off the floor," he said. "It was the eighties, I was a teenager, but I remember it: they put us all in the back."
> **Kip Brown Former Trump Castle Employee**

In 1993, Trump wanted to open a casino in Connecticut, that would compete with one owned by the Mashantucket Pequot Nation. While testifying, he told the House sub-committee on Native American Affairs that the mafia had infiltrated Indian casinos. To this day, 20 years later, there is zero evidence of these claims. Here are some highlights from his remarks:

"They don't look like Indians to me... They don't look like Indians to Indians."

Asked what an Indian looks like, Trump said:

"You know ... you know."

"An Indian chief is going to tell Joey Killer to please get off his reservation? It's unbelievable to me."

"It's obvious that those so-called Indians have done a major number on his head,"

"No one's more for the Indians than Donald Trump."

This comment drew laughter.

The Washington Post, October 6, 1993

"I think Eminem is fantastic, and most people think I wouldn't like Eminem. And did you know my name is in more black songs than any other name in hip-hop? Black entertainers love Donald Trump. Russell Simmons told me that."

Playboy, 2004

"I'll shake hands. I shake hands with people. But it's not something I like — look, I'm not a huge fan of Japan, but I love their custom."
Larry King Live, May 17, 2005

"I know the Chinese. I've made a lot of money with the Chinese. I understand the Chinese mind."
Xinhua, April 2011

"I did very well with Chinese people. Very well. Believe me."
TIME, April 14, 2011

Robert LiButti, a Mob-linked felon — who was a Trump Plaza high-roller — was apparently known at the casino for berating women and people of color in slur-filled tirades. The Trump Plaza was fined $200,000 in 1991 for instructing black employees not to go near LiButti. —
Huffington Post, March 8, 2016

"I have a great relationship with the blacks. I've always had a great relationship with the blacks."
Albany's Talk 1300, April 14, 2011

"It's like in golf. A lot of people -- I don't want this to sound trivial -- but a lot of people are switching to these really long putters, very unattractive. It's weird. You see these great players with these really long putters, because they can't sink three-footers anymore. And, I hate it. I am a traditionalist. I have so many fabulous friends who happen to be gay, but I am a traditionalist."
New York Times, May 2011

Donald Trump explaining his stance on gay marriage?

"Well, you know, when it comes to racism and racists, I am the least racist person there is. And I think most people that know me would tell you that. I am the least racist, I've had great relationships," Trump said. "In fact, Randall Pinkett won, on the as you know, on 'The Apprentice' a little while ago, a couple of years ago. And Randall's been outstanding in every way. So I mean, I am the least racist person."
Fox & Friends, May 2011

"The concept of global warming was created by and for the Chinese in order to make U.S. manufacturing non-competitive."
Twitter, Nov. 6, 2012

"I promise you that I'm much smarter than Jonathan Leibowitz - I mean Jon Stewart @TheDailyShow. Who, by the way, is totally overrated."
Twitter, April 24, 2013

"If Jon Stewart is so above it all & legit, why did he change his name from Jonathan Leibowitz? He should be proud of his heritage!"
Twitter, May 3, 2013

"According to Bill O'Reilly, 80% of all the shootings in New York City are blacks — If you add Hispanics, that figure goes to 98%, 1% white."
Twitter, June 5, 2013

"Sadly, the overwhelming amount of violent crime in our major cities is committed by blacks and hispanics-a tough subject-must be discussed."
Twitter, June 5, 2013

"Sadly, because president Obama has done such a poor job as president, you won't see another black president for generations!"
Twitter, November 25, 2014

"I'm a negotiator like you folks,"

**Republican Jewish Committee Event
March 12, 2015**

"Is there anyone in this room who doesn't negotiate deals? Probably more than any room I've ever spoken."
**Republican Jewish Committee Event
March 12, 2015**

"You're not going to support me even though I'll be the best guy for Israel,"
**Republican Jewish Committee Event
March 12, 2015**

"I believe I could bring the two sides [Israel and Palestine] together. It would take six months."
"I don't know that Israel has the commitment to make it,"
Republican Jewish Committee Event
March 12, 2015

"Our great African American President hasn't exactly had a positive impact on the thugs who are so happily and openly destroying Baltimore!"
Twitter, April 28, 2015

"When Mexico sends its people, they're not sending the best. They're sending people that have lots of problems and they're bringing those problems. They're bringing drugs, they're bringing crime. They're rapists and some, I assume, are good people, but I speak to border guards and they're telling us what we're getting."
Trump Tower, June 16, 2015

"They're sending us not the right people. It's coming from more than Mexico. It's coming from all over South and Latin America, and it's coming probably from the Middle East."
Trump Tower, June 16, 2015

"Likewise, tremendous infectious disease is pouring across the border. The United States has become a dumping ground for Mexico and, in fact, for many other parts of the world."
Trump Tower, June 16, 2015

"I will build a great wall – and nobody builds walls better than me, believe me – and I'll build them very inexpensively. I will build a great, great wall on our Southern border, and I will make Mexico pay for that wall. Mark my words."
Trump Tower , June 16, 2015
Announcing his candidacy

"Islamic terrorism is eating large portions of the Mideast. They've become rich. I'm in competition with them."
Trump Tower , June 16, 2015

He's in competition with the terrorists because they have become rich? Competition for what…The Forbes List?

"What can be simpler or more accurately stated? The Mexican Government is forcing their most unwanted

people into the United States. They are, in many cases, criminals, drug dealers, rapists, etc."
Press Statement, July 6, 2015

Clarifying his comments of June 16, 2015, Trump takes a cheap shot at Univision for dropping the Miss USA pageant and severing their relationship with the Latinophobe...

"Interestingly, Univision has just announced they are attempting to go public despite very poor and even negative earnings, which is not a good situation for a successful IPO or high stock price —not to mention that I am currently suing them for breach of contract. Remember, Univision is the one who began this charade in the first place, and they are owned by one of Hillary Clinton's biggest backers. After the speech was made, there were numerous compliments and indeed, many rave "reviews"—there was very little criticism. It wasn't until a week after my announcement that people started to totally distort these very easy to understand words. If there was something stated incorrectly, it would have been brought up immediately and with great enthusiasm."

I think his "Mexicans are rapists" comment was met with great "enthusiasm!"

"A nation WITHOUT BORDERS is not a nation at all. We must have a wall. The rule of law matters. Jeb just doesn't get it."
Twitter, July 28, 2015

> "Russia's borders don't end anywhere!"
> — Vladimir Putin

"People say you don't like China. No, I love them. I beat China all the time."
Trump Tower, June 16, 2015

"And if you look at black and African American youth, to a point where they've never done more poorly. There's no spirit."
The Independent, June 24, 2015

"Well if you look at the statistics of people coming, you look at the statistics on rape, on crime, on everything coming in illegally into this country it's mind-boggling!"
CNN: The Situation Room, July 1, 2015

Trump said his information came from a Fusion article — but he misread the story. Don Lemon corrected him, and pointed out that Fusion's figures show 80 percent of women and girls from Central America are victims of rape while immigrating to the United States.

To which Trump replied...

"Well, somebody's doing the raping, Don. I mean somebody's doing it. Who's doing the raping? Who's doing the raping?"
CNN, July 1, 2015

The National Sex Offender website statistics show that, 66% of rapists are white.

"You know who owns Fusion?" Trump said. "Univision! Go to Fusion and pick up the stories on rape. It's unbelievable when you look at what's going on. So all I'm doing is telling the truth."
CNN, July 1, 2015

"I don't have a racist bone in my body."
Entertainment Tonight, July 1, 2015

"They don't feel the same way I do about illegal immigration. One of the things that has always bothered me, and it haunts me, is what China is doing with their currency manipulation. They make my ties and they make my shirts, and I've always hated it. So I said to Macy's, 'Let's just forget it.'"
    CNN, July 1, 201

"We are disappointed and distressed by recent remarks about immigrants from Mexico. We do not believe the disparaging characterizations portray an accurate picture of the many Mexicans, Mexican Americans and Latinos who have made so many valuable contributions to the success of our nation," Macy's said. "In light of statements made by Donald Trump, which are inconsistent with Macy's values, we have decided to discontinue our business relationship with Mr. Trump and will phase-out the Trump menswear collection, which has been sold at Macy's since 2004."
    Press Release, July 1, 2015

"Jeb Bush has to like the Mexican Illegals because of his wife."
    Twitter, July 4, 2015

"I'll win the Latino vote because I'll create jobs. I'll create jobs and the Latinos will have jobs they didn't have."
NBC News, July 8, 2015

> "Donald Trump has had several foreign wives. It turns out that there are really are jobs Americans won't do."
>
> –Mitt Romney

"Hey, about those killer Mexicans…" Trump went to CNN and spoke to Jake Tapper. Enjoy…

"I like Mexico, I love the Mexican people. I do business with the Mexican people, but you have people coming through the border that are from all over. And they're bad. They're really bad."

"You have people coming in, and I'm not just saying Mexicans — I'm talking about people that are from all over that are killers and rapists, and they're coming into this country."

"The Mexican government forces many bad people into our country. Because they're smart. They're smarter than our leaders."
NBC News, July 8, 2015

"I'll do better on that vote than anybody. I will win that vote. I have a great relationship with the Mexican people. They love me, I love them."
NBC News, July 8, 2015

On an episode of All-Star Celebrity Apprentice, which aired in early 2013, Lil Jon bought and wore an Uncle Sam costume during one of the show's competitions. When Trump heard about Lil Jon's efforts, the mogul began jokingly referring to the rapper as "Uncle Tom" to Apprentice staffers, not realizing that "Uncle Sam" was a patriotic mascot and "Uncle Tom" was a racial epithet.

"We kept trying to explain to [Trump] that that's not a word you can use, that it's offensive," an Apprentice employee told The Daily Beast. "One of the executive producers had to call him up directly to [plead with] him not to say it, and Trump was like, 'No, that's a saying, it's Uncle Tom.' There are several takes in the footage of the dailies that has him trying to figure out the difference between 'Uncle Tom' and Uncle Sam. He just couldn't grasp that it was offensive… When [Trump] decides he wants to do something, that's his way."
Rolling Stone, October 15, 2016

"The U.S. will invite El Chapo, the Mexican drug lord who just escaped prison, to become a U.S. citizen because our "leaders" can't say no!"
Twitter, July 13, 2015

"I will build the best wall, the biggest, the strongest, not penetrable, they won't be crawling over it, like giving it a little jump and they're over the wall, it costs us trillions"
NH1, July 20, 2015

"And, you know, I have a great relationship with African Americans, as you possibly have heard. I just have great respect for them and you know they like me.."
CNN, July 23, 2015

"They say this is what's happening because our leaders are stupid, our politicians are stupid; And the Mexican government is much smarter, much sharper, much more cunning."…"They send the bad ones over, because they don't want to pay for them, they don't want to take care of them. Why should they, when the stupid leaders of the United States will do it for 'me?"
First Presidential Debate, August 6, 2015

"Jeb Bush will not be able to negotiate against Mexico. Jeb Bush with Mexico said, 'People, come in,' they come in, it's an act of love, OK?"
Birch Run Michigan, Aug. 11, 2015

"I'm leading in the Hispanic vote, and I'm going to win the Hispanic vote. I'm also leading in the regular vote."
Birch Run Michigan, August 11, 2015

Trump's message for Muslims: "We love you, we want to work with you, we want you to turn in the bad ones, we want you to practice vigilance, we know that if you know a lot, in many cases, we want you to turn in the bad ones. We all want to get along. We want to get back to a normal, peaceful life."
MSNBC Morning Joe, August 12, 2015

"@YoungYoung54: @JeriHyatt @megynkelly @JebBush So true. Jeb Bush is crazy, who cares that he speaks Mexican, this is America, English !!"
Twitter, August 24, 2015

"When these people walk into the room," Trump began. "They don't say, 'Oh hello, how's the weather? It's so beautiful outside. How are the Yankees doing? They're doing wonderful, that's great.' They say (mimicking a broken English accent and squinting his face), 'We want deal!'"
Iowa Speech, August 26, 2015

"We have to have a wall. We have to have a border. And in that wall we're going to have a big fat door where people can come into the country, but they have to come in legally."
Late Show with Stephen Colbert, September 2015

"Donald J. Trump is calling for a complete and total shutdown of Muslims entering the United States until our country's representatives can figure out what the hell is going on."
Charleston SC, December 2015

"Now Donald said he wants to run for President and move on into the White House. Why not? It wouldn't be the first time he pushed a black family out of their home.

– Snoop Dog

"Until we are able to determine and understand this problem and the dangerous threat it poses, our country cannot be the victims of horrendous attacks by people that believe only in jihad, and have no sense of reason or respect for human life,"
Waterloo Iowa, December 7, 2015

> Yahoo News asked Trump whether his push for increased surveillance of American Muslims could include warrantless searches. He suggested he would consider a series of drastic measures.
>
> "We're going to have to do things that we never did before. And some people are going to be upset about it, but I think that now everybody is feeling that security is going to rule," Trump said. "And certain things will be done that we never thought would happen in this country in terms of information and learning about the enemy. And so we're going to have to do certain things that were frankly unthinkable a year ago."
>
> Yahoo News asked Trump whether this level of tracking might require registering Muslims in a database or giving them a form of special identification that noted their religion. He wouldn't rule it out.
>
> "We're going to have to — we're going to have to look at a lot of things very closely," Trump said when presented with the idea. "We're going to have to look at the mosques. We're going to have to look very, very carefully."
> **Yahoo News, November 19, 2015**

A day after a black activist was kicked and punched by voters at a Donald Trump rally in Alabama, Trump tweeted an image packed with racially loaded and incorrect murder statistics.

The image shows a masked, dark-skinned man with a handgun and a set of points, ostensibly about deaths in 2015:

"Blacks killed by whites -- 2%"
"Blacks killed by police -- 1%"
"Whites killed by police -- 3%"
"Whites killed by whites -- 16%"
"Whites killed by blacks -- 81%"
"Blacks killed by blacks -- 97%'

The image cites the "Crime Statistics Bureau - San Francisco" which does not exist.

The most glaring inaccuracies have to do with white homicide victims. Trump cast blacks as the primary killers of whites, but the exact opposite is true. By overwhelming percentages, whites tend to kill other whites. Similarly, blacks tend to kill other blacks. These trends have been observed for decades.

POLITIFACT, November 23, 2015

"I have many friends who are Muslims. They're phenomenal people. They are so happy at what I'm doing."
CNN, December 10, 2015

Your Muslim friends are happy with your Muslim ban?

"I love the Middle East. I love the people of the Middle East."
CNN, December 10, 2015

"You know where things bother me?; If things are true. If that were true, it would bother me tremendously. But of course if you were a racist you probably wouldn't care. But if things are true, it would bother me. But if it's so false, and honestly I don't hear it often."
CNN, December 10, 2015

On being likened to Hitler...His grammar fascinates me.

"We can't continue to allow China to rape our country"
Ft. Wayne Indiana, May 1, 2016

Ahhh, I see....China is doing the raping. Got it Don?

"What do I know about it? All I know is what's on the Internet."
Meet the Press, March 13, 2016

After a protester rushed the stage at one of his rallies, Trump tweeted out a video tying the protester to ISIS. The video, of course, was debunked.

"The LGBT community, the gay community, the lesbian community — they are so much in favour of what I've been saying over the last three or four days. Ask the gays what they think and what they do, in, not only Saudi Arabia, but many of these countries, and then you tell me — who's your friend, Donald Trump or Hillary Clinton?"
Atlanta, June 15, 2016

"What do you have to lose by trying something new like Trump? What do you have to lose? You're living in poverty; your schools are no good; you have no jobs; 58 percent of your youth is unemployed. What the hell do you have to lose?" –Donald Trump, making a pitch to win over African American voters, adding, "At the end of four years, I guarantee you that I will get 95 percent of the African-American vote."
Dimondale Michigan, August 19, 2016

> Perfect Obama's dad born in Africa, Mitt Romney's dad born in Mexico. Any pure breeds left? #CNNDebate
> **Twitter, January 19, 2012**
>
> This corrupt country has a head Negro in charge. What is he doing for blk children? He's helping everybody else,Why?
> **Twitter, March 3, 2013**
>
> **—Katrina Pierson**
> **Trump Campaign Spokeswoman**

"Appreciate the congrats for being right on radical Islamic terrorism, I don't want congrats, I want toughness & vigilance. We must be smart!"
Twitter, June 12, 2016

Trump's humble/braggy response to the Orlando nightlclub massacre. My question to Donald is, "Who congratulated you? Hmmmm?"

"I've been treated very unfairly by this judge. Now, this judge is of Mexican heritage. I'm building a wall, OK? I'm building a wall."
CNN interview, June 5, 2016

"Happy Cinco de Mayo! The best taco bowls are made in Trump Tower Grill. I love Hispanics!"
Twitter, May 5, 2016

In the interest of full disclosure, I should tell you that I actually looked up the date for this quote....I felt like such a moron!

"I'll take jobs back from China, I'll take jobs back from Japan. The Hispanics are going to get those jobs, and they're going to love Trump."
Laredo Texas, July 23, 2015

"I'm doing good for the Muslims. Many Muslim friends of mine are in agreement with me. They say, 'Donald, you brought something up to the fore that is so brilliant and so fantastic."
CNN, December 9, 2015

> "Analysts say Hillary Clinton's plan to defeat Donald Trump involves painting Trump as 'dangerous and bigoted.' She plans on doing this by quoting Trump accurately."
> —Conan O'Brien

"We have a protester! By the way, were you paid $1,500 to be a thug?"…"Throw him out! Throw him out!"
Kinston North Carolina, October 26, 2016

Donald Trump addressing a black man in the crowd of a rally — the "thug" was a Trump supporter.

"Saudi Arabia and China: They all buy apartments from me. They pay millions and millions of dollars. Am I supposed to hate them? I love them! I sell apartments for $50 million, $30 million, $25 million, $18 million, some of the cheap ones, like $10 million, OK? Those are the cheap ones. I don't even sign those contracts."
New Hampshire, 2015

July 6, 2015
Statement from Donald J. Trump:

I don't see how there is any room for misunderstanding or misinterpretation of the statement I made on June 16th during my Presidential announcement speech. Here is what I said, and yet this statement is deliberately distorted by the media:

"When Mexico (meaning the Mexican Government) sends its people, they're not sending their best. They're not sending you (pointing to the audience). They're not sending you (pointing again). They're sending people that have lots of problems, and they're bringing those problems to us. They're bringing drugs. They're bringing crime. They're rapists. And some, I assume, are good people! But I speak to border guards and they tell us what we're getting. And it only makes common sense. They're sending us not the right people. It's coming from more than Mexico. It's coming from all over South and Latin America, and it's coming probably from the Middle East. But we don't know. Because we have no protection and we have no competence, we don't know what's happening. And it's got to stop and it's got to stop fast."

What can be simpler or more accurately stated? The Mexican Government is forcing their most unwanted people into the United States. They are, in many cases, criminals, drug dealers, rapists, etc. This was evident just this week when, as an example, a young woman in San Francisco was viciously killed by a 5 time deported Mexican with a long criminal record, who was forced back into the United States because they didn't want him in Mexico. This is merely one of thousands of similar incidents throughout the United States. In other words, the worst elements in Mexico are being pushed into the United States by the Mexican government.

The largest suppliers of heroin, cocaine and other illicit drugs are Mexican cartels that arrange to have Mexican immigrants trying to cross the borders and smuggle in the drugs. The Border Patrol knows this.

Likewise, tremendous infectious disease is pouring across the border. The United States has become a dumping ground for Mexico and, in fact, for many other parts of the world. On the other hand, many fabulous people come in from Mexico and our country is better for it. But these people are here legally, and are severely hurt by those coming in illegally. I am proud to say that I know many hard working Mexicans—many of them are working for and with me…and, just like our country, my organization is better for it.

The Mexican Government wants an open border as long as it's a ONE WAY open border into the United States. Not only are they killing us at the border, but they are killing us on trade … and the country of Mexico is making billions of dollars in doing so.

I have great respect for Mexico and love their people and their peoples' great spirit. The problem is, however, that their leaders are far smarter, more cunning, and better negotiators than ours. To the citizens of the United States, who I will represent far better than anyone else as President, the Mexican government is not our friend…and why should they be when the relationship is totally one sided in their favor on both illegal immigration and trade. I have pointed this out during my speeches and it is something Mexico doesn't want me to say. In actuality, it was only after my significant rise in the polls that Univision, previously my friend, went ballistic. I believe that my examples of bad trade deals for the United States was of even more concern to the Mexican government than my talk of border security.

I have lost a lot during this Presidential run defending the people of the United States. I have always heard that it is very hard for a successful person to run for President. Macy's, NBC, Serta and NASCAR have all taken the weak and very sad position of being politically correct even though they are wrong in terms of what is good for our country. Univision, because 70% of their business comes from Mexico, in my opinion, is being dictated to by the Mexican Government. The last thing Mexico wants is Donald Trump as President in that I will make great trade deals for the United States and will have an impenetrable border--only legally approved people will come through easily.

Interestingly, Univision has just announced they are attempting to go public despite very poor and even negative earnings, which is not a good situation for a successful IPO or high stock price—not to mention that I am currently suing them for breach of contract. Remember, Univision is the one who began this charade in the first place, and they are owned by one of Hillary Clinton's biggest backers. After the speech was made, there were numerous compliments and indeed, many rave "reviews"—there was very little criticism. It wasn't until a week after my announcement that people started to totally distort these very easy to understand words. If there was something stated incorrectly, it would have been brought up immediately and with great enthusiasm.

The issues I have addressed, and continue to address, are vital steps to Make America Great Again! Additionally, I would be the best jobs President that God ever created. Let's get to work!

"What I won't do is take in two hundred thousand Syrians who could be ISIS"
Face the Nation, CBS, 2015

> "You're going to have to watch and study the mosques, because a lot of talk is going on in the mosques," he said on MSNBC's "Morning Joe" early Monday.
>
> "And from what I heard, in the old days — meaning a while ago — we had a great surveillance going on in and around the mosques of New York City," the outspoken billionaire added.
>
> Trump then said that the U.S. would have "absolutely no choice" besides shutting down mosques when "some bad things happen."
> **The Hill, November 19, 2015**

"They're [Syrian refugees] going to be gone. They will go back. ... I've said it before, in fact, and everyone hears what I say, including them, believe it or not," Trump said of the refugees. "But if they're here, they have to go back, because we cannot take a chance. You look at the migration, it's young, strong men. We cannot take a chance that the people coming over here are going to be ISIS-affiliated."
Yahoo News, November 19, 2015

> Yahoo News has reported that about half of the approximately 2,000 refugees from Syria who have come to the U.S. so far have been children. Another quarter are more than 60 years old. The Obama administration has maintained that the extensive screening process for these refugees makes the program safe to maintain — not to mention a reflection of America's core values.

"Bing bing, bong bong, bing bing bing"
Lincoln Day speech, 2015

"He has done nothing for African-Americans. You look at what's gone on with their income levels. You look at what's gone on with their youth. I thought that he would be a great cheerleader for this country. I thought he'd do a fabulous job for the African-American citizens of this country. He has done nothing."

This Week, 2015

The History of The Donald and David Duke

1991

Larry King: Did the David Duke thing bother you? Fifty-five percent of the whites in Louisiana voted for him.

Trump: I hate seeing what it represents, but I guess it just shows there's a lot of hostility in this country. There's a tremendous amount of hostility in the United States.

King: Anger?

Trump: It's anger. I mean, that's an anger vote. People are angry about what's happened. People are angry about the jobs. If you look at Louisiana, they're really in deep trouble. When you talk about the East Coast, it's not the East Coast. It's the East Coast, the middle coast, the West Coast...

Larry King Live, November 19, 1991

2000

"The Reform Party now includes a Klansman, Mr. Duke, a neo-Nazi, Mr. [Patrick] Buchanan, and a communist, Ms. [Lenora] Fulani. This is not company I wish to keep."
**Statement From Donald Trump
February 13, 2000**

Matt Lauer: When you say the party is self-destructing, what do you see as the biggest problem with the Reform Party right now?

Trump: Well, you've got David Duke just joined — a bigot, a racist, a problem. I mean, this is not exactly the people you want in your party.
NBC's Today Show, February 14, 2000

Take note: Trump knows who David Duke is in 1991 and 2000

2015

John Heilemann: How do you feel about the David Duke quasi-endorsement?

Trump: I don't need his endorsement; I certainly wouldn't want his endorsement. I don't need anyone's endorsement.

Heilemann: Would you repudiate David Duke?

Trump: Sure, I would do that, if it made you feel better. I don't know anything about him. Somebody told me yesterday, whoever he is, he did endorse me. Actually I don't think it was an endorsement. He said I was absolutely the best of all of the candidates.
Bloomberg Politics, August 26, 2015

2016

"Voting for these people [Marco Rubio and Ted Cruz], voting against Donald Trump at this point is really treason to your heritage. I'm not saying I endorse everything about Trump, in fact I haven't formally endorsed him. But I do support his candidacy, and I support voting for him as a strategic action. I hope he does everything we hope he will do."
David Duke, on his radio program
February 25, 2016

Question: How do you feel about the recent endorsement from David Duke?

Trump: I didn't even know he endorsed me. David Duke endorsed me? Okay, all right. I disavow, okay?
Press Conference, February 26, 2016

Jake Tapper: I want to ask you about the Anti-Defamation League, which this week called on you to publicly condemn unequivocally the racism of former KKK grand wizard David Duke, who recently said that voting against you at this point would be 'treason to your heritage.' Will you unequivocally condemn David Duke and say that you don't want his vote or that of other white supremacists in this election?

Trump: Well, just so you understand, I don't know anything about David Duke. Okay? I don't know anything about what you're even talking about with white supremacy or white supremacists. So, I don't know. I don't know, did he endorse me or what's going on, because, you know, I know nothing about David Duke. I know nothing about white supremacists. And so you're asking me a question that I'm supposed to be talking about people that I know nothing about.

Tapper: But I guess the question from the Anti-Defamation League is, even if you don't know about their endorsement, there are these groups and individuals endorsing you. Would you just say unequivocally you condemn them and you don't want their support?

Trump: Well, I have to look at the group. I mean, I don't know what group you're talking about. You wouldn't want me to condemn a group that I know nothing about. I would have to look. If you would send me a list of the groups, I will do research on them. And, certainly, I would disavow if I thought there was something wrong.

Tapper: The Ku Klux Klan?

Trump: But you may have groups in there that are totally fine, and it would be very unfair. So, give me a list of the groups, and I will let you know.

Tapper: Okay. I mean, I'm just talking about David Duke and the Ku Klux Klan here, but…"

Trump: I don't know any — honestly, I don't know David Duke. I don't believe I have ever met him. I'm pretty sure I didn't meet him. And I just don't know anything about him.

Tapper: All right.
CNN's State of the Union, February. 28, 2016

Trump: "I'm sitting in a house in Florida, with a very bad earpiece that they gave me, and you could hardly hear what he was saying. But what I heard was 'various groups.' And I don't mind disavowing anybody and I disavowed

David Duke. And I disavowed him the day before at a major news conference.... I have no problem disavowing groups, but I'd at least like to know who they are. It would be very unfair to disavow a group if the group shouldn't be disavowed. I have to know who the groups are. But I disavowed David Duke."

NBC's Today Show, February 29, 2016

George Stephanopoulos: So, are you prepared right now to make a clear and unequivocal statement renouncing the support of all white supremacists?

Trump: Of course, I am. I mean, there's nobody that's done so much for equality as I have. You take a look at Palm Beach, Florida, I built the Mar-a-Lago Club, totally open to everybody; a club that frankly set a new standard in clubs and a new standard in Palm Beach and I've gotten great credit for it. That is totally open to everybody. So, of course, I am."

**ABC's Good Morning America
March 1, 2016**

"I think profiling is something that we're going to have to start thinking about as a country."

"You look at Israel and you look at others, and they do it and they do it successfully. And you know, I hate the concept of profiling, but we have to start using common sense,"

Face the Nation, June 20, 2016

Trump's answer when asked if he supported increased profiling of Muslims in America.

In March, a group of 30 black students were removed from a Trump rally at Valdosta State University in Valdosta, GA. The students were reportedly standing silently in the bleachers, but were asked to leave.

"We didn't plan to do anything," said Tahjila Davis, a 19-year-old mass media major. "They said, 'This is Trump's property; it's a private event.' But I paid my tuition to be here."

"At a Donald Trump rally the other night, a supporter shouted out the Nazi salute 'Sieg Heil!' Trump immediately responded, 'There is no place for that here – save it for my inauguration.'"
—**Conan O'Brien**

After a man wearing a turban was reportedly escorted out of a Donald Trump rally, the Republican presidential candidate asked: "He wasn't wearing one of those hats, was he?"

The man was ejected from the rally at Muscatine High School, Iowa, on Sunday, after standing up with a sign reading "Stop Hate" as Mr Trump was speaking about the 11 September terror attacks and the San Bernardino shooting.

The businessman then pointed to the man, saying: "He wasn't wearing one of those hats, was he?

"Was he wearing one of those things? And he never will, and that's okay because we got to do something folks because it's not working."
The Independent, January 25, 2016

"A protester had to be escorted out of a Donald Trump rally last night for yelling, 'Trump's a racist.' The protester was removed because the Trump campaign has that phrase copyrighted."
—Seth Meyers

TRUMP
Commandeer-in-Chief

"There's nobody bigger or better at the military than I am"

"What does it all mean when some wacko over in Syria can end the world with nuclear weapons?"
New York Times, April 8, 1984

Speaking of some wacko with nuclear weapons...

> "Several months ago, a foreign policy expert on the international level went to advise Donald Trump. And three times [Trump] asked about the use of nuclear weapons. Three times he asked at one point if we had them why can't we use them,"
>
> **—Joe Scarborough**
> **MSNBC Morning Joe**

"It would take an hour and a half to learn everything there is to learn about missiles. ... I think I know most of it anyway."
Washington Post, November 15, 1984

"When the students poured into Tiananmen Square, the Chinese government almost blew it. Then they were vicious, they were horrible, but they put it down with strength. That shows you the power of strength. Our country is right now perceived as weak ... as being spit on by the rest of the world"
Playboy Interview, 1990

Touting the "power of strength" used against the student protesters...hundreds (some estimate thousands) of civilians were killed for a pro-democracy protest....and to think..."the Chinese government almost blew it."

"I think if this country gets any kinder or gentler, it's literally going to cease to exist."
Playboy, 1990

"President Trump would believe very strongly in extreme military strength. He wouldn't trust anyone. He wouldn't trust the Russians; he wouldn't trust our allies; he'd have a huge military arsenal, perfect it, understand it."
Playboy, March 1990

In "an hour and a half" apparently...

"I've always thought about the issue of nuclear war; it's a very important element in my thought process. It's the ultimate, the ultimate catastrophe, the biggest problem this world has, and nobody's focusing on the nuts and bolts of it. It's a little like sickness. People don't believe they're going to get sick until they do. Nobody wants to talk about it. I believe the greatest of all stupidities is people's believing it will never happen, because everybody knows how destructive it will be, so nobody uses weapons. What bullshit."
Playboy, 1990

[If conflict between Japan and nuclear-armed North Korea were to break out] "it would be a terrible thing, but if they do, they do"."Good luck," Trump added. "Enjoy yourself, folks."
Rothschild WI, April 7, 2016

"Who else in public life has called for a pre-emptive strike on North Korea?"
The America We Deserve, July 2, 2000

Nobody Donald...nobody...

"Look at Putin -- what he's doing with Russia -- I mean, you know, what's going on over there. I mean this guy has done -- whether you like him or don't like him -- he's doing a great job in rebuilding the image of Russia and also rebuilding Russia period."
Larry King Live, October 2007

> According to a new poll that just came out, Vladimir Putin's approval rating in Russia has reached an all-time high. Putin is polling well among Russians who don't want to be killed.
> — **Conan O'Brien**

"Our weak President, that kisses everybody's ass, is in more wars than I have ever seen. Now he's in Libya, he's in Afghanistan, he's in Iraq. Nobody respects us."
Las Vegas Speech, April 29, 2011

"We build a school, we build a road, they blow up the school, we build another school, we build another road they blow them up, we build again, in the meantime we can't get a fucking school in Brooklyn."
Las Vegas, April 28, 2011

He's not wrong.

"I rented him a piece of land. He paid me more for one night than the land was worth for two years, and then I didn't let him use the land. **That's what we should be doing.** I don't want to use the word 'screwed', but I screwed him."
Fox News, March 21, 2011

Trump explains how he will approach foreign relations through this example concerning a deal he made with Muammar Qaddafi.

About OPEC: "We have nobody in Washington that sits back and said, you're not going to raise that fucking price."
Las Vegas Speech, April 29, 2011

Trump vastly over-estimates an American President's power to control oil prices. The US only consumes about 20% and only holds about 2% of the reserves...

About China: "Listen you motherfuckers, we're going to tax you 25 percent!"
Las Vegas Speech, April 29, 2011

One, Trump built his Vegas building with illegal Chinese steel and two, his clothing line is manufactured in China.

"We have weak, pathetic leadership. Our leaders are stupid, they are stupid people."
Las Vegas Speech, April 29, 2011

"Our president will start a war with Iran because he has absolutely no ability to negotiate. He's weak and ineffective, so the only way he figures to get re-elected, and as sure as you're sitting there, is to start a war with Iran."
YouTube, 2011

"You stay and protect the oil and you take the oil and you take whatever's necessary for them and you take what's necessary for us and we pay ourselves back 1.5 trillion or more. We take care of Britain and you take care of other countries that helped us and we don't be so stupid. You know, we're the only country, if you look at wars over the years, and I study wars, okay? My whole life is a war. You look at wars over the years. A country goes in, they conquer and they stay. We go in, we conquer and then we leave. And we hand it to people that we don't even know. Now, who are the people that are going to be running Iraq? The person that hates the United States the most will be

running Iraq. So, in a nutshell, we go in, we take over the second largest oil fields and we stay."
O'Reilly Factor, March 31, 2011

The Plan: annex the Middle East and take their oil...and he wonders why they don't like us!

"You know what the Arab League is? Saudi Arabia and a couple of others of the richest nations in the world. They said, 'We want you to go into Libya. We don't like Qaddafi. Get rid of Qaddafi.' Why aren't they paying for this?"
O'Reilly Factor, March 31, 2011

"This guy got the Nobel Peace Prize and every time I look is he's going into another country."
O'Reilly Factor, March 31, 2011

Never mind that two out of the three wars Obama finds himself in were started years before he became President.

"Putin has big plans for Russia. He wants to edge out its neighbors so that Russia can dominate oil supplies to all of Europe. I respect Putin and Russians but cannot believe

our leader (Obama) allows them to get away with so much...Hats off to the Russians."
Time to Get Tough, December 2011

> Vladimir Putin has singled out Donald Trump as someone he could "get along with very well." Mussolini and Hitler were also pretty tight.
> — **Warren Holstein**

"Do you think Putin will be going to The Miss Universe Pageant in November in Moscow - if so, will he become my new best friend?"
Twitter, June 18, 2013

The only thing worse than seeing Vladimir Putin horseback riding topless, is seeing Donald Trump join in

"I would like to extend my best wishes to all, even the haters and losers, on this special date, September 11th."
Twitter, 8:12 PM - 11 Sep 2013

"I think he's done really a great job of outsmarting our country."
Larry King Live, October 2013

This comment was in response to Putin successfully arranging with the US for the removal of Syria's chemical weapons, to avert US airstrikes.

"Isn't it interesting that immediately after September 11th, everybody was asking for, and indeed demanding, torture of any kind. No reports!"
Twitter, December 12, 2014

"I do know what to do and I would know how to bring ISIS to the table or, beyond that, defeat ISIS very quickly. **And I'm not gonna tell you what it is tonight**…. If I win, I don't want the enemy to know what I'm doing. Unfortunately, I'll probably have to tell at some point, but there is a method of defeating them quickly and effectively and having total victory…. All I can tell you is that it is a foolproof way of winning the war with ISIS and it will 100% — at a minimum they'll come to the table and actually they'll be defeated very quickly."
Fox News, May 27, 2015

> It's 1968 and Richard Nixon is running against LBJ on a promise to bring a quick end to the Vietnam war. When reporters pressed him for details he would pat his suit coat pocket and say he had a "secret plan" for victory.
>
> **Diogenes Bartleby**
> **The Daily Kos**

"There is a way of beating ISIS so easily, so quickly and so effectively and it would be so nice.... I know a way that would absolutely give us absolute victory … **The problem is people will take the idea and run with it and forget where it came from....** I ran it past two or three people. [It's] so simple. It's like the paper clip. You know, somebody came up with the idea of the paper clip and made a lot of money and everybody's saying, 'Boy, why didn't I think of that, it's so simple.' This is so simple, so surgical, it would be an unbelievable thing. Now, I've been around saying this, you would think somebody from the administration would at least call me and say, 'Hey, could you tell us what it is?' It happens to be a great idea. But at the right time, I guess I'll give it."
Simon Conway Show, June 3, 2015

His biggest concern is getting credit for his "plan"...of course, as we later learn, he had no plan at all.

Charles Krauthammer said that Donald Trump's proposed plan to defeat ISIS is "not much of a plan."

Trump said that on the first day of his presidency he'll call on his top generals to submit within 30 days a "plan for soundly and quickly defeating ISIS."

"You get Trump saying that he has a plan for ISIS," Krauthammer said on Special Report. "And the plan is to ask for a plan when he gets into office. That's not much of a plan."

He continued: "And considering that he would ask for the plan from the generals, whom he say know less about ISIS than he does. I think it's more an exercise in remarkable humility on his part than it is in grand strategy."

Fox News Insider, September 7, 2016

"Saudi Arabia without us is gone. They're gone."
Trump Tower, June 16, 2015

"There's nobody bigger or better at the military than I am"
O'Reilly Factor, June 16, 2015

> "I say that knowing every time his name is said out loud, he has a shattering orgasm... Donald Trump is America's back mole. It may have seemed harmless a year ago, but now that it's become frighteningly bigger, it's no longer wise to ignore it."
>
> **–John Oliver**

"Putin has no respect for our president whatsoever. He's got a tremendous popularity in Russia, they love what he's doing, they love what he represents. I was over in Moscow two years ago and I will tell you – you can get along with those people and get along with them well. You can make deals with those people. Obama can't."
O'Reilly Factor, June 16, 2015

> Russia has named Vladimir Putin "Man of the Year" for the 15th year in a row. Putin got 143 million votes, and the guy he was up against got killed in a mysterious boating accident.
>
> **— Conan O'Brien**

"I would be willing to bet I would have a great relationship with Putin; It's about leadership."
O'Reilly Factor, June 16, 2015

"The other candidates — they went in, they didn't know the air conditioning didn't work. They sweated like dogs. They didn't know the room was too big because they didn't have anybody there. How are they gonna beat ISIS? I don't think it's gonna happen."

Announcement Speech, June 16, 2015

> "I ask Allah to deliver America to Trump," an ISIS spokesman wrote last week on an ISIS-affiliated outlet.
>
> Another extremist posted on various ISIS social media channels that "The 'facilitation' of Trump's arrival in the White House must be a priority for jihadists at any costs!" the magazine reported.
>
> **New York Daily News, August 27, 2016**

"People say 'you don't like China.' No, I love them. But their leaders are much smarter than our leaders. And we can't sustain ourselves with that. It's like, take the New England Patriots and Tom Brady and have them play your high school football team."

Announcement Speech, June 16, 2015

"I know the smartest negotiators in the world. I know the good ones, I know the bad ones, I know the overrated ones. You got a lot of them that are overrated. They're not good, they think they are, they get good stories, cause the newspapers get buffaloed. But they're not good. But I know the best negotiators in the world. I'd put them one for each country. Believe me, folks, we'd do very well."
Announcement Speech, June 16, 2015

"I will stop Iran from getting nuclear weapons. And we won't be using a man like Secretary Kerry that has absolutely no concept of negotiation, who's making a horrible and laughable deal, who's just being tapped along as they make weapons right now and then goes into a bicycle race at 72-years-old and falls and breaks his leg. I won't be doing that. And I promise, I will never be in a bicycle race — that I can tell you."
Announcement Speech, June 16, 2015

Please insert your own Trump small-penis/bicycle shorts joke here.

"I would bomb the hell out of those oilfields. I wouldn't send many troops because you won't need 'em by the time I'm finished."
CNN, July 10, 2015

230

"John McCain is not a war hero. … He is a war hero because he was captured. I like people who weren't captured, OK?"
			Ames, Iowa, July 18, 2015

Possibly the most ignorant thing Trump has ever said. But, I like his medal for neatness.

CBS 60 MINUTES
INTERVIEW WITH SCOTT PELLEY

PELLEY: We're at war with ISIS as we sit here. How do you end it?

TRUMP: I would end ISIS forcefully. I think ISIS, what they did, was unbelievable what they did with James Foley and with the cutting off of heads of everybody, I mean these people are totally a disaster. Now, let me just say this, ISIS in Syria, Assad in Syria, Assad and ISIS are mortal enemies. We go in to fight ISIS. Why aren't we letting ISIS go and fight Assad and then we pick up the remnants? Why are we doing this? We're fighting ISIS and Assad has to be saying to himself, "They have the nicest or dumbest people that I've ever imagined."

PELLEY: Let me get this right, so we lay off ISIS for now?

TRUMP: Excuse me, let —

PELLEY: Lay off in Syria, let them destroy Assad. And then we go in behind that?

TRUMP: –that's what I would say. Yes, that's what I would say…. If you look at Syria. Russia wants to get rid of ISIS. We want to get rid of ISIS. Maybe let Russia do it. Let 'em get rid of ISIS. What the hell do we care?
CBS 60 Minutes, September 27, 2015

There it is…his masterplan to defeat ISIS quickly, "100%" that he was afraid would be stolen from him.

"My number was so incredible, and it was a very high draft number. Anyway, so I never had to do that [the Vietnam War]."
**Never Enough: Donald Trump and the
Pursuit of Success
September 22, 2015**

> Trump also insisted that he had actually known military life. In a separate conversation he said, "I always thought I was in the military." He said that in prep school he received more military training than most actual soldiers did, and he had been required to live under the command of men such as Ted Dobias who had been real officers and soldiers. "I felt like I was in the military in a true sense," added Trump, "because I dealt with the people."
>
> **Never Enough: Donald Trump and the Pursuit of Success**
> **— Michael D'Antonio**

"There were people that were cheering on the other side of New Jersey, where you have large Arab populations. They were cheering as the World Trade Center came down."
Campaign Rally, November, 2015
Nope.

"With the terrorists, you have to take out their families. When you get these terrorists, you have to take out their families. They care about their lives, don't kid yourselves. But they say they don't care about their lives. You have to take out their families."
Fox & Friends, December 2, 2015

War crimes-shmore crimes!

"@thumpmomma: I likewise saw militant Muslims burning our flag and burning George Bush photos and figures, right after 9/11! Not#here!"
Twitter, December 2, 2015

"I will be so good at the military your head will spin."
The Hugh Hewitt Show, September 3, 2015

My head is spinning already...

> "By the way, Donald, it's pronounced 'huge,' not 'eyuge.' Also, it's pronounced 'I am fucking delusional,' not 'I am running for President.'"
> —Seth McFarlane

"I watched when the World Trade Center came tumbling down. And I watched in Jersey City, New Jersey, where thousands and thousands of people were cheering as that building was coming down. Thousands of people were cheering,"
Birmingham AL, November 21, 2015

Fact Check:

The next day, on ABC This Week with George Stephanopoulos, noting that Trump was in Manhattan the morning of the attack, and that **"the police say that didn't happen."** — in truly Trumpianesque defiance of the evidence, Trump doubled-down on his claims and said:

"It was on television. I saw it. It was well covered at the time, George. Now, I know they don't like to talk about it, but it was well covered at the time. There were people over in New Jersey that were watching it, a heavy Arab population, that were cheering as the buildings came down. Not good."
ABC This Week with George Stephanopoulos
November 22, 2015

It did not happen.
It's a debunked conspiracy theory

"I know more about ISIS than the generals do, believe me...I would bomb the shit out of them."
CNN, November 13, 2015

The generals or ISIS?

> At a campaign rally, Donald Trump said he would "bomb the shit" out if ISIS. It's all part of his new campaign slogan, "Donald Trump: The Drunk Guy Next to You at the Sports Bar."
> — **Conan O'Brien**

"I'm the worst thing that's ever happened to ISIS."
Barbara Walters, December 2015

And America, and television, and Atlantic City, and hairspray, and tanning beds and pussies...

"I think I'd get along very well with Vladimir Putin. I just think so."
Reuters, Scotland, July 31, 2015

I think so too....and I find it troubling

"I think the biggest thing we have is that we were on '60 Minutes' together [Trump and Putin] and we had fantastic ratings. One of your best-rated shows in a long time; So that was good, right? So we were stable mates."
Face the Nation Oct. 11, 2015

They appeared on the same show, but were interviewed in different countries by different journalists...and never met.

"I think that I would probably get along with him [Putin] very well. And I don't think you'd be having the kind of problems that you're having right now."
Face the Nation Oct. 11, 2015

"But, as far as the Ukraine is concerned, and you could Syria — as far as Syria, I like — if Putin wants to go in, and I got to know him very well because we were both on 60 Minutes, we were stablemates, and we did very well that night."
GOP Debate, Milwaukee Nov. 10, 2015:.

> "I never met Putin, I don't know who Putin is. He said one nice thing about me. He said I'm a genius."
> ### CNN, July 27, 2016

Actually, Putin said Trump was "flamboyant" — and watch this lie grow and morph for the rest of the chapter...

"But I'm good at war, had a lot of wars of my own. I'm really good at war. I love war — in a certain way — but only when we win."
Fort Dodge IA, November 12, 2015

Twitter wars with Rosie O'Donnell and Cher are not the same thing. The audience of active duty soldiers know that better than anybody.

"It is always a great honour to be so nicely complimented by a man so highly respected within his own country and beyond. I have always felt that Russia and the United States should be able to work well with each other towards defeating terrorism and restoring world peace, not to mention trade and all of the other benefits derived from mutual respect."
Press Statement
December 17, 2015

Trump blushing like a schoolgirl after Putin praise

"Would I approve waterboarding? You bet your ass I would. In a heartbeat. I would approve more than that. It works… and if it doesn't work, they deserve it anyway for what they do to us".
Columbus Ohio, November 23, 2015

When it was pointed out that soldiers cannot carry out orders that are illegal, or contravene The Geneva Conventions or the War Crimes Act, Trump appeared to be non-plussed:

"They're not going to refuse me. Believe me."
Columbus Ohio, November 23, 2015

Referring to his military commanders obeying his instructions…

"We're losing a lot of people because of the Internet. We have to go see Bill Gates and a lot of different people that really understand what's happening. We have to talk to them about, maybe in certain areas, closing that Internet up in some way. Somebody will say, 'Oh freedom of

speech, freedom of speech.' These are foolish people. We have a lot of foolish people."
Rally in Mt. Pleasant SC, December 8, 2015

America doesn't control the Internet on foreign soil; Bill Gates is retired and cures malaria now — and an Internet blackout in conflict areas would leave the US Military without vital communications and intelligence capabilities....plus, without Internet, how would the Donald Tweet about Katie Perry, The New York Times and Bette Midler?

MSNBC'S MORNING JOE

MIKA: Do you like Vladimir Putin's comments about you?

TRUMP: Sure, when people call you brilliant that's always good, especially when the person heads up Russia.

SCARBOROUGH: Yeah, well also, it's a person who kills journalists and political alli…I mean, political opponents and invades countries, obviously uhh…that would be a concern, would it not?

TRUMP: At least he's running his country and at least he's a leader, unlike what we have in this country.

SCARBOROUGH: Yeah, but, again, he kills journalists that don't agree with him.

TRUMP: Yeah, well, I think our country does plenty of killing also Joe. Ya know...(crosstalk)

SCARBOROUGH: What....what... do you mean by that?

TRUMP: There's a lot of stupidity going on in the world...a lot of killing going on, a lot of stupidity..and that's uhh..the way it is. But you didn't ask me the question. You asked me a different question, and so that's fine.
MSNBC, December 18, 2015

> Donald Trump said that "nobody has proven that Putin killed anyone." Unfortunately, all of the journalists who could do that are dead.
> — **Adam Wolf**

> "CNN says that Trump's top priorities aren't jobs, or the economy, and sure as hell not reproductive rights or reducing carbon emissions. To give you an idea, waterboarding makes the list, right below building the Infamous Wall and improving ties with Russia." (repeal Obamacare was #1)
>
> **Esquire, November 9, 2016**

"I would bring back waterboarding and I'd bring back a hell of a lot worse than waterboarding."
Republican Debate ABC News, February 6, 2016.

"He completely misunderstands the military profession that he would head if he were the president," said Robert Killebrew, a retired colonel who served in the Army for more than 30 years. Others were less polite. In a pair of ads produced by the American Future Fund, a retired Special Forces commander named Michael Waltz calls Trump a draft-dodger who "hasn't served this country a day in his life," and a Vietnam veteran, Tom Hanton, says that Trump's quip about POWs was "the most infuriating comment I think I've heard from a politician in my entire life." One former Marine infantry officer described Trump to me as a "fake-bake-ing chicken hawk" "He completely misunderstands the military profession that he would head if he were the president," said Robert Killebrew, a retired colonel who served in the Army for more than 30 years. Others were less polite. In a pair of ads produced by the American Future Fund, a retired Special Forces commander named Michael Waltz calls Trump a draft-dodger who "hasn't served this country a day in his life," and a Vietnam veteran, Tom Hanton, says that Trump's quip about POWs was "the most infuriating comment I think I've heard from a politician in my entire life." One former Marine infantry officer described Trump to me as a "fake-bake-ing chicken hawk" whose "knowledge of the Middle East could be trumped (sorry) by your average Georgetown sophomore.

—Andy Kroll, The Huffington Post

"If you look at North Korea – this guy [Kim Jong Un], he's like a maniac, OK? And you have to give him credit. How many young guys — he was like 26 or 25 when his father died — take over these tough generals, and all of a sudden — you know, it's pretty amazing when you think of it. How does he do that? Even though it is a culture and it's a cultural thing, he goes in, he takes over, and he's the boss. It's incredible. He wiped out the uncle. He wiped out this one, that one. I mean, this guy doesn't play games. "
Iowa Rally, January 9, 2016

He didn't "take over these tough generals," he executed them in a political purge in 2014.

Kim Jong-un's uncle was arrested and executed in 2013. Kim Jong-un also executed Jang's family, to completely destroy all traces of Jang's existence through "extensive executions." Those put to death included the children and grandchildren of all close relatives. Some of the people reportedly killed in Kim's purge include Jang's sister, her husband and his nephew. The nephew's two sons were also said to have been killed. At the time of Jang's removal, it was announced that "the discovery and purge of the Jang group ... made our party and revolutionary ranks purer ..." and after his execution, state media warned that the army "will never pardon all those who disobey the order of the Supreme Commander."

"I could stand in the middle of Fifth Avenue and shoot somebody, and I wouldn't lose any voters, okay? It's, like, incredible."
Sioux Center Iowa, January 23, 2016

Yes, it's, like, totally incredible…

> "Donald Trump has claimed that his candidacy is fuelling more interest in voting. More people are signing up to vote. Just like herpes fuels more interest in Valtrex, for instance."
>
> **—Jimmy Kimmel**

"The wife knew exactly what was happening. They left two days early with respect to the World Trade Center and they went back to where they went and they watched their husband on television flying into the World Trade Center, flying into the Pentagon, and probably trying to fly into the White House, except we had some very, very brave souls on that third plane. All right? I have no problem with it."
Detroit MI, March 3, 2016

According to the 9/11 Commission Report, only two of the hijackers were married, and there is no evidence that either of the wives had ever traveled to the United States, much less left the U.S. two days before the attacks.

"I think Islam hates us. There's a tremendous hatred. We have to get to the bottom of it. There is an unbelievable hatred of us."
CNN, Anderson Cooper, March 9, 2016.

MORNING JOE

MIKA: Dire foreign policy issues percolating around the world right now, who are you consulting with consistently, so that you're ready on Day One?

TRUMP: I'm speaking with myself, number one, because I have a very good brain, and I've said a lot of things....I know what I'm doing and I listen to a lot of people, I talk to a lot of people and at the appropriate time I'll tell you who the people are. But my primary consultant is myself and I have a good instinct for this stuff.
MSNBC, March 16, 2016

"'Yeah! OK! That sounds good!' So now the obvious question is, will he ever not win? Yes, Trump is unstoppable. He's like Godzilla with less foreign policy experience."

–Stephen Colbert

"I actually think I'd be a great cheerleader – beyond other things, the other things that I'd do – I actually think I'd be a great cheerleader for the country."
The Washington Post, March 21, 2016

> "That's what he's best at. Putting a bow on a turd, marking up the price, and selling it so hard, you want it —even though you know it's just a turd with a bow on it. America is that turd!"
>
> **—Lewis Black**

INTERVIEW WITH FRED HIATT

TRUMP: We should have never been in Iraq. It was a horr- it was one of the worst decisions ever made in the history of our country. We then got out badly, then after we got out, I said, "Keep the oil. If we don't keep it Iran's going to get it." And it turns out Iran and ISIS basically—

HIATT: How do you keep it without troops, how do you defend the oil?

TRUMP: You would… You would, well for that– for that, I would circle it. I would defend those areas.

HIATT: With U.S. troops?

TRUMP: Yeah, I would defend the areas with the oil. And I would have taken out a lot of oil. And, uh, I would have kept it. I mean, I would have kept it, because, look: Iran has the oil, and they're going to have the oil, well, the stuff they don't have, because Iran is taking over Iraq as sure as you're sitting there.
    The Washington Post, March 21, 2016

                        Wait For It…

                                        Okay, turn the page.

MORNING JOE - August 3, 2016

SCARBOROUGH: What concerns you most about Donald Trump?

GEN. MICHAEL HAYDEN: How erratic he is, Joe. I can argue about this position or that position. I do that with the current president. But he's inconsistent, and when you're the head of a global superpower, inconsistency, unpredictability, those are dangerous things. They frighten your friends and they tempt your enemies. And so I would be very, very concerned.

HAROLD FORD JR.: General Hayden, Harold Ford, very, very quickly. Who amongst your peers that you respect greatly, whether they think like you or not think like you, that you know that's advising Mr. Trump?

HAYDEN: No one.

MIKE BARNICLE: That's a good answer.

SCARBOROUGH: I have to follow up with that, I'll be careful here. Several months ago, a foreign policy expert on the international level went to advise Donald Trump, and three times he asked about the use of nuclear weapons. Three times he asked, at one point, "If we have them, why can't we use them?"

BARNICLE: Wow.

SCARBOROUGH: That's one of the reasons why he has — he just doesn't have foreign policy experts around him.

BARNICLE: Trump? Trump asked three times whether we can use nuclear weapons?

SCARBOROUGH: Three times in an hour briefing, "Why can't we use nuclear weapons?"

Esquire, November 9, 2016

"I'm never going to rule anything out—I wouldn't want to say. Even if I wasn't, I wouldn't want to tell you that because at a minimum, I want them to think maybe we would use them,"

Bloomberg, March 23, 2016

BIDEN: I showed Trump the nuclear launch codes before he left.
OBAMA: Joe, that was your old GameBoy...
BIDEN: God damn right!

"Who knows?" –Donald Trump, when asked if he would start a war with China as president

New York Times, March 25, 2016

"Trump is kind of like the movie Snakes on a Plane. Sure the idea is entertaining. But an actual snake on your plane would be terrifying. And that's what's happening now. The plane is American democracy. And the snake is Trump."-

–Seth Meyers

INTERVIEW WITH ANDERSON COOPER

COOPER: So if you said, Japan, yes, it's fine, you get nuclear weapons, South Korea, you as well, and Saudi Arabia says we want them, too?

TRUMP: Can I be honest with you? It's going to happen, anyway. It's going to happen anyway. It's only a question of time. They're going to start having them or we have to get rid of them entirely. But you have so many countries already, China, Pakistan, you have so many countries, Russia, you have so many countries right now that have them.
Now, wouldn't you rather in a certain sense have Japan have nuclear weapons when North Korea has nuclear weapons? And they do have them. They absolutely have them. They can't — they have no carrier system yet but they will very soon.
Wouldn't you rather have Japan, perhaps, they're over there, they're very close, they're very fearful of North Korea, and we're supposed to protect.

CNN, March 29, 2016

I think anyone who listens to what Donald Trump has to say on foreign policy should be concerned. This is not the first time that he has talked about nuclear weapons in a reckless manner. Remember, he was interested in maybe having Japan or South Korea leave the U.S. nuclear umbrella and develop nuclear weapons of their own. That is contrary to decades' worth of nuclear weapons policy and is, frankly, a terrible and dangerous idea.

— **John Noonan to Slate Aug 3/2016**

"(The San Bernardino attackers) had bombs on the floor. Many people saw this. Many, many people. Muslims living with them in the same area. They saw that house. They say that," Trump said. "One didn't want to turn -- he said, 'I don't want to turn him in because I don't want to be accused of racial profiling.' He saw bombs all over the apartment, OK? It's just an excuse."

Republican Town Hall Milwaukee
March 29, 2016

There was no evidence to support these claims.

"It was 67 years, or it's over 60 years old. It is -- many countries, doesn't cover terrorism. OK? It covers the Soviet Union, which is no longer in existence. And NATO has to either be rejiggered, changed for the better."

Republican Town Hall Milwaukee
March 29, 2016

NATO "doesn't cover terrorism?"...After the al Qaeda terrorist attacks of September 11, 2001. NATO lead the military intervention in Afghanistan. In October 2011, they launched Operation Active Endeavour, which has NATO patrolling the Mediterranean and monitoring shipping "to help deter, defend, disrupt and protect against terrorist activity." In 2004, NATO's Defence Against Terrorism Program was launched. This involves sharing "...military innovations to protect troops, civilians and critical infrastructure against suicide attacks, improvised explosive devices (IEDs), rocket attacks against aircraft and helicopters and attacks using chemical, biological or radiological material." NATO also adopted counterterrorism policy guidelines and created a Center for Excellence focused on Defence Against Terrorism — So, yeah, NATO doesn't "cover terrorism."

INTERVIEW WITH CHRIS MATHEWS

TRUMP: I don't think I — well, someday, maybe.

MATTHEWS: When? Maybe?

TRUMP: Of course. If somebody —

MATTHEWS: Where would we drop — where would we drop a nuclear weapon in the Middle East?

TRUMP: Let me explain. Let me explain.
Somebody hits us within ISIS — you wouldn't fight back with a nuke?

...

MATTHEWS: OK. The trouble is, when you said that, the whole world heard it. David Cameron in Britain heard it. The Japanese, where we bombed them in '45, heard it. They're hearing a guy running for president of the United States talking of maybe using nuclear weapons. Nobody wants to hear that about an American president.

TRUMP: Then why are we making them? Why do we make them?

MSNBC, March 30, 2016

> "Nuclear deterrence is about balance. Trump is an elephant jumping up and down on one side of the scale. So damn dangerous."
> —**John Noonan, Twitter, Aug 3/16**
> FMR Air Force/Policy Advisor
> He actually sat at the buttons.

"Japan is better if it protects itself against this maniac of North Korea. We are better off frankly if South Korea is going to start protecting itself ... they have to protect themselves or they have to pay us."

Anderson Cooper 360, March 29, 2016

The Danger of Ignorance

> "Earlier this week, Trump raised eyebrows and startled Japan and South Korea, two of America's strongest allies, with the suggestion that the U.S. military should be withdrawn from their shores, with nuclear weapons replacing them."
> **CNN Politics, April 2, 2016**

BLITZER: But—but you're ready to let Japan and South Korea become nuclear powers?

TRUMP: I am prepared to—if they're not going to take care of us properly, we cannot afford to be the military and the police for the world.
CNN, May 4, 2016

> "The person who made the statements doesn't know much about foreign policy or nuclear policy or the Korean Peninsula or the world generally."
> — **President Barack Obama**

INTERVIEW WITH CHRIS WALLACE

WALLACE: You want to have a nuclear arms race on the Korean peninsula?

TRUMP: In many ways, and I say this, in many ways, the world is changing. Right now, you have Pakistan and you have North Korea and you have China and you have Russia and you have India and you have the United States and many other countries have nukes.

WALLACE: Understood.

TRUMP: It's not like, gee whiz, nobody has them.
Fox News, April 3, 2016

> Experts say that one of the biggest threats facing Donald Trump's presidency could be North Korea. Evidently, Kim Jong-un is so incompetent and unstable, they are worried Trump will give him a cabinet post.
> — Conan O'Brien

"The father of the Orlando shooter was a Taliban supporter from Afghanistan, one of the most repressive anti-gay and anti-women regimes on Earth."
New York, June 22, 2016

The father of Orlando shooter, Omar Mateen, is not a supporter of the Taliban. He told CNN that he has been a longtime opponent of terrorism. CNN also translated the videos Seddique Mateen posted to YouTube and found no evidence of Taliban support. The elder Mateen lumps ISIS, al Qaeda and the Taliban all together as terrorists. In his interview with CNN, he called the groups "the enemy of humanity."

"Saddam Hussein was a bad guy, right? ... But you know what he did well? He killed terrorists. He did that so good. They didn't read 'em the rights, they didn't talk. They were a terrorist, it was over."
Raleigh, NC, July 6, 2016

How I imagine Darth Vader would praise Saddam Hussein.

"Hillary Clinton invented ISIS with her stupid policies. She is responsible for ISIS. She led Barack Obama, because I don't think he knew anything. I think he relied on her."
60 Minutes, July 17, 2016

"America is far less safe and the world is far less stable than when Obama made the decision to put Hillary Clinton in charge of America's foreign policy. I am certain it is a decision he truly regrets… This is the legacy of Hillary Clinton: death, destruction and terrorism and weakness."
RNC July 22, 2016

"Go look at the graves of brave patriots who died defending the United States of America," Khizr Khan said, addressing Trump. "You will see all faiths, genders and ethnicities. You have sacrificed nothing and no one."

— **Khizr Khan, Gold Star Dad**

"I think I've made a lot of sacrifices. I work very, very hard. I've created thousands and thousands of jobs, tens of thousands of jobs, built great structures. I've had tremendous success. I think I've done a lot."
ABC News, July 30, 2016

> "They are self-serving half-truths from a self-serving half-man who has somehow convinced half the country that sacrifice is the same thing as success."
> — John Oliver

"I always wanted to get the Purple Heart. This was much easier."
Ashburham Rally, August 2, 2016

It's got to be better than the shrivelled little black one he has now.

Trump got his Purple Heart the same way he got his wealth...someone handed it to him.

"ISIS is honoring President Obama. He is the founder of ISIS. He is the founder of ISIS, okay? He is the founder. He founded ISIS. And I would say the co-founder would be crooked Hillary Clinton."
Broward County, August 10, 2016

"He knows what he's saying when he says Obama founded ISIS. And he doesn't care that it's wrong. He just cares that people talk about it... 'Trump, you've got one star on Yelp.' 'Yes, but look how many reviews!'"

—Trevor Noah
The Daily Show

CNBC'S SQUAWK BOX

WAPNER: I want to ask you about the rally last night in Florida that you referenced where you called the president of the United States the founder of ISIS, you said it repeatedly. ... Do you think it's appropriate to call the sitting president of the United States the founder of a terrorist organization that wants to kill Americans?"

TRUMP: He was the founder of ISIS, absolutely."

"Why is there something wrong with saying that? Are people complaining that I said he was the founder of ISIS?"

CNBC, August 11, 2016

THE HUGH HEWITT SHOW

HEWITT: I've got two more questions. Last night, you said the President was the founder of ISIS. I know what you meant. You meant that he created the vacuum, he lost the peace.

TRUMP: No, I meant he's the founder of ISIS. I do. He was the most valuable player. I give him the most valuable player award. I give her, too, by the way, Hillary Clinton.

HEWITT: But he's not sympathetic to them. He hates them. He's trying to kill them.

TRUMP: I don't care. He was the founder. His, the way he got out of Iraq was that that was the founding of ISIS, okay?

Hugh Hewitt, August 11, 2016

Stop trying Hugh, nuance is over Trump's head.

> "At a rally over the weekend, Donald Trump was surrounded by Secret Service agents after a man tried to rush the stage. The Secret Service said the man was dangerous and disturbed, but they had to protect him anyway. Proving once and for all, the best way to keep everyone safe and sound is to build a wall around Donald Trump."
>
> –Jimmy Fallon

"Iraq and Iran were very similar militarily, and they'd fight, fight, fight, and then they'd rest. They'd fight, fight, fight, and then Saddam Hussein would do the gas, and somebody else would do something else, and they'd rest."
Virginia Beach, VA September 6, 2016

Trump demonstrating how he's so "good at the military that your head will spin"

> "Today is the Republican caucus in Nevada, and Donald Trump is projected to win. When asked why they're voting for him, Americans said, 'We're used to doing things in Nevada that we'll regret tomorrow.'"
>
> **—Conan O'Brien**

COMMANDER-IN-CHIEF FORUM
with Matt Lauer

TRUMP: Sure. I mean, part of the problem that we've had is we go in, we defeat somebody, and then we don't know what we're doing after that. We lose it, like as an example, you look at Iraq, what happened, how badly that was handled. And then when President Obama took over, likewise, it was a disaster. It was actually somewhat stable.

I don't think could ever be very stable to where we should have never gone into in the first place.

But he came in. He said when we go out — and he took everybody out. And really, ISIS was formed. This was a terrible decision. And frankly, we never even got a shot. And if you really look at the aftermath of Iraq, Iran is going to be taking over Iraq. They've been doing it. And it's not a pretty picture.

The — and I think you know — because you've been watching me I think for a long time — I've always said, shouldn't be there, but if we're going to get out, take the oil. If we would have taken the oil, you wouldn't have ISIS, because ISIS formed with the power and the wealth of that oil.

LAUER: How were we going to take the oil? How were we going to do that?

TRUMP: Just we would leave a certain group behind and you would take various sections where they have the oil.

They have — people don't know this about Iraq, but they have among the largest oil reserves in the world, in the entire world.

And we're the only ones, we go in, we spend $3 trillion, we lose thousands and thousands of lives, and then, Matt, what happens is, we get nothing. You know, it used to be to the victor belong the spoils. Now, there was no victor there, believe me. There was no victor. But I always said: Take the oil.

September 8, 2016

ISIS got its start, and its oil from Syria — just sayin'

"When Iran, when they circle our beautiful destroyers with their little boats, and they make gestures at our people that they shouldn't be allowed to make, they will be shot out of the water."

Pensacola, Florida, September 9, 2016

> This guy [Trump] is dangerously unhinged. And, for all the things people have said about me over the years, I should be able to spot Dangerously Unhinged.
>
> —Glenn Beck

"When people come back from war and combat — and they see things that maybe a lot of the folks in this room have seen many times over, and you're strong and you can handle it, but a lot of people can't handle it. And they see horror stories. They see events that you couldn't see in a movie. Nobody would believe it."
**Retired American Warriors PAC Event,
October 3, 2016**

Remarks on PTSD...

DOOCY: So, Mr. Trump, the president called for more gun controls. He also said it was terror and he said it was a hate crime -- but he did not say that it was Islamic terrorism. And for that reason, you say he should quit.

TRUMP: He doesn't get it or he gets it better than anybody understands -- it's one or the other, and either one is unacceptable.
Fox and Friends, June 13, 2016

No, you read that right. Trump implied that President Obama is a terrorist. This, regarding the Orlando Nightclub Shootings

"I've been right about a lot of things. I don't want congratulations. What I want them to do is be tough and vigilant, our government. Look guys, we're led by a man that either is not tough, not smart or has something else in mind. And the something else in mind -- people can't believe it. People cannot believe that President Obama is acting the way he acts and can't even mention the words radical Islamic terrorism. There's something going on. It's inconceivable. There's something going on."
Fox and Friends, June 13, 2016

To avoid stoking Islamaphobia, the term used now is "Radical Jihadists" That's why he doesn't mention "the words."....and don't believe him...
He really does want congratulations.

"Appreciate the congrats for being right on radical Islamic terrorism, I don't want congrats, I want toughness & vigilance. We must be smart!"
Tweet about the Orlando nightclub massacre, June 12, 2016

> "Say what you will about Trump, he is not stupid. He is a smart man with a deep understanding of what stupid people want."
> — **Andy Borowitz**

"I'll tell you one thing, this is a very good looking group of people here. Could I just go around so I know who the hell I'm talking to?"
The Washington Post, 2016

Responding to a question about using nuclear weapons against ISIS from a member of the Washington Post Editorial Board

"How about bringing baskets of money into Iraq? I want to know -- who were the soldiers who had that job? I want to know who were the soldiers that had that job, 'cause I think they're living well right now, whoever they may be."
North Carolina, June 14, 2016

Trump is doubling down on a previous accusation...

> "I want to know who are the soldiers carrying suitcases with $50m?" asked Trump. "How stupid are we? I wouldn't be surprised if those soldiers, if the cash didn't get there."
> — **Donald Trump**
> **Keene NH, October 1, 2015**

Every week I would sit for hours, listening as my interpreters relayed the heartbreaking stories of mothers, fathers and widows. They showed me their scars and pictures of the piles of bricks that used to be their homes. It felt good to help those I could, and gut-wrenching to turn down those I couldn't. I spent much of a year of my life inside an aluminum trailer, far away from my friends and family, missing holidays and birthdays, trying to block out the speaker that would blare "Incoming! Incoming!" as mortars flew into the base while I tried to sleep.

In the course of my mission, we carried with us U.S. cash. A lot of U.S. cash. When the year was up, we had distributed about $2 million to the people of Iraq for justified damage. I personally never took a dime. No one else from my team took anything, either. The accounting measures put in place by the finance department made that all but impossible, and, frankly, the thought of stealing never even entered our minds. The core values of the Army are loyalty, duty, respect, selfless service, honour, integrity and personal courage; those words are something that my team and I took very seriously.

**--Corbin Reiff, The Washington Post
June 16, 2016**

"[Vladimir Putin} is not going into Ukraine, OK, just so you understand. He's not gonna go into Ukraine, all right? You can mark it down. You can put it down."
ABC's This Week, July 31, 2016

It WAS marked down; in about 1000 newspapers back in 2014, when it happened.

"Russia, if you're listening, I hope you're able to find the 30,000 emails that are missing. I think you will probably be rewarded mightily by our press."
Doral Florida, July 27, 2016

Sure Donald, publicly hope that Vladimir Putin gains access to classified government information.

> "Stupid presidents, smart presidents, white presidents, black presidents — doesn't work! What this country needs is a crazy Third World dictator. And Donald Trump has what it takes to be that. He's already got a plane with his name on it, solid gold buildings, a harem…"
> **—Lewis Black**

> Russian President Vladimir Putin appeared on a call-in show for Russian television and he actually took questions. It was really fun — the most common question Putin got was, "Will I ever see my family again?"
>
> **— Conan O'Brien**

"I have no relationship with him other than he called me a genius. He said Donald trump is a genius and he is going to be the leader of the party and he's going to be the leader of the world or something." [Trump embellished] "These characters that I'm running against said, 'We want you to disavow that statement.' I said what, he called me a genius, I'm going to disavow it? Are you crazy? Can you believe it? How stupid are they."

"And besides that wouldn't it be good if we actually got along with countries. Wouldn't it actually be a positive thing. I think I'd have a good relationship with Putin. I mean who knows."

Fox News, O'Reilly Factor, April 28, 2016

Actually, Putin called Trump "flamboyant," but the story keeps getting more elaborate with every telling.

"I'm saying that I'd possibly have a good relationship [with Putin]. He's been very nice to me. If we can make a great deal for our country and get along with Russia that would be a tremendous thing. I would love to try it."
Fox News, O'Reilly Factor, April 28, 2016

"I never met Putin, I don't know who Putin is."
Doral Florida, July 27, 2016

"We don't even really know who the leader [of ISIS] is."
Fox News, May 5, 2016

We do. His name is Abu Bakr al-Baghdadi

> Donald Trump said that he'll be the biggest threat to ISIS. Does that mean he's running for president of ISIS too?
> — **Seth Meyers**

FOX NEWS - INTERVIEW WITH BRET BAIER

BAIER: About Russia, you were asked yesterday if you've ever spoken to Vladimir Putin. And you said, 'I don't want to say.'

TRUMP: Yes, I have no comment on that. No comment. I was in Russia —

BAIER: But one of the things people like about you is to answer any question.

TRUMP: Yes. But I don't — let's assume I did. Perhaps it was personal. You know I don't want to — I don't want to hurt his confidence. But I know Russia well. I had a major event in Russia two or three years ago. Miss Universe contest which was a big, big incredible event, an incredible success.

BAIER: OK. So we can say you talked to him.

TRUMP: No. I got to meet a lot of people…

Fox News, May 5, 2016

"If Russia or any other country or person has Hillary Clinton's 33,000 illegally deleted emails, perhaps they should share them with the FBI!

Twitter, July 27, 2016

"CLINTON'S CLOSE TIES TO PUTIN DESERVE SCRUTINY"
Twitter, October 4, 2016

Give me a break!

"I was shocked to hear [Vladimir Putin] mention the N-word. You know what the N-word is. Number one he doesn't like him and number two he doesn't respect him. I think he's going to respect your president if I'm elected and I hope he likes me."
Doral FL, July 27, 2016

> "We've said it many times before, President Putin has never had any contacts with Trump, never spoken to him, including by telephone," Dmitry Peskov said. "The same goes for all of his staff."

"I would treat Vladimir Putin firmly, but there's nothing I can think of that I'd rather do than have Russia friendly, as opposed to the way they are right now, so that we can go and knock out ISIS with other people."
News Conference, July 28, 2016

"I'm not going to tell Putin what to do. Why would I tell him what to do?"
News Conference, July 28, 2016

"Why do I have to get tough on Putin? I don't know anything other than that he doesn't respect our country.
News Conference, July 28, 2016

Yes, please vote for the guy who doesn't know anything!

"President Trump would be so much better for US-Russian relations. It can't be worse. I don't think he has any respect for Clinton. I think he respects me. I think it would be great to get along with him."
News Conference, July 28, 2016

> Russian President Vladimir Putin said that he may seek a fourth presidential term. Putin added, "But that's for the people to decide" — then he laughed for ten minutes.
>
> **— Conan O'Brien**

"I think under the leadership of Barack Obama and Hillary Clinton, the generals have been reduced to rubble."
"They have been reduced to a point where it's embarrassing to our country. ... And I can just see the great, as an example, Gen. George Patton spinning in his grave as ISIS, we can't beat."
Commander-In-Chief Forum
September 8, 2016

Carnegie-Mellon studied the candidates' grammar (among other things) and concluded that Trump speaks at a fifth grade level. To put that in terms Trump will understand...

You have a yuge problem with the talking. Your sentences are bigly confusing and end badly...ironically, I believe your presidency will end that same way.

"Whatever you think about Marco Rubio and Ted Cruz, at least you basically know where they stand, but Trump's opinions have been wildly inconsistent. He's been pro-choice and pro-life, for and against assault weapon bans, in favour of both bringing Syrian refugees and deporting them out of the country, and that inconsistency has been troubling…This is the frontrunner for the Republican nomination advocating a war crime. And he might say he was joking or he's changed his mind about any of these things, and private individuals are allowed to change their minds — we all do it — but when he's sworn in as president on Jan. 20, 2017, on that day, his opinions are going to matter. And you will remember that date, because it's the one that time travellers from the future will come back to try and stop the whole thing from happening."

—**John Oliver**

TRUMP
CONTRADICTOR-IN-CHIEF

What I say is what I say.

Donald Trump has a fluid and flexible relationship with the truth. What Donald believes is coloured constantly by his immediate goals and his environment. The truth is whatever serves him best in the moment. Setting aside his big, fat, hairy, pants-on-fire lies…of which there are many. What I see in the contradictions here is a man who is so shallow that he doesn't know his own mind. He is not self-aware. We have a four-year-old at home who does this. A young child sees what he wants or needs right now and acts upon this. It's developmental and he will grow out of it.

However, we shouldn't hold out any hopes that The Donald is going to spontaneously evolve as a human being and become honest and capable of internal reflection. I believe this is likely owing to a serious psychiatric condition or defect of personality.

What I see in these quotes — especially the ones that involve the books — is the author's notion of what Donald should be saying or thinking. We are getting — through no fault of their own — business advice from the writers, not from Trump and that is possibly why some of the contradictions come about.

Apparently Donald is a notoriously difficult man to interview. His attention span is so short that he becomes restless after a few questions, he is resistant to speaking about the past, and he doesn't comprehend — seriously, his mind goes blank — when given a question that delves even slightly beneath his orange-stained veneer.

So, I don't categorize these contradictions in the same way that I do his big, fat lies. I see them as evidence that Donald Trump is fundamentally and inexorably superficial and incapable of self-regulation — and thus, he retains the freewheeling relationship to reality of a preschooler.

I have to admit, and it's important to note, that the following list of contradictions came from an article on POLITICO.com.

While I curated the list a bit and made some changes, the heavy-lifting was done by Michael Kruse and Noah Weiland.

I don't expect much from my little self-published tome, so I didn't ask for reprint permissions…and I didn't use the article in it's entirety either….and there is the matter of the material I took being quotes from The Donald.

Basically, I don't know if I stepped on any toes to get here. But, I do thank them for all of their research and organization, for it helped shape my research and organization.

I find myself reading Michael Kruse quite often, so I recommend his articles highly.

This is my little way of saying….Michael, Noah, please don't be mad!

If you are, email me and we'll work it out.

Best Wishes,

Jules Carlysle.

"I have no intention of running for president."
Time, September 14, 1987

"I am officially running for president."
New York, June 16, 2015

If you asked me in 1987, I would have told you that I had no intention of writing a book about Donald Trump....stuff changes.

"I wanted to do this for myself. ... I had to do it for myself."
Time, August 18, 2015

"I don't want it for myself. I don't need it for myself."
ABC News, November 20, 2015

"Politicians are all talk and no action."
Twitter, May 27, 2015

"I'm no different than a politician running for office."
New York Times, July 28, 2015

"I'm not a politician."
CNN, August 11, 2015

"If I ever ran for office, I'd do better as a Democrat than as a Republican—and that's not because I'd be more liberal, because I'm conservative."
Playboy, March 1990

"I'm a registered Republican. I'm a pretty conservative guy. I'm somewhat liberal on social issues, especially health care."
CNN, October 8, 1999

"You'd be shocked if I said that in many cases I probably identify more as a Democrat."
CNN, March 21, 2004

"Look, I'm a Republican. I'm a very conservative guy in many respects—I guess in most respects."
The Hugh Hewitt Show, February 25, 2015

"I've actually been an activist Democrat and Republican."
CNN, October 8, 1999

"Folks, I'm a conservative, but at this point, who cares? We got to straighten out the country."
Burlingame, California, April 29, 2016

"I'm totally pro-choice."
Fox News, October 31, 1999

"I'm pro-life."
CPAC, February 10, 2011

"Look, I'm very pro-choice. I hate the concept of abortion. I hate it. I hate everything it stands for. I cringe when I listen to people debating the subject, but you still—I just believe in choice. ... I am strongly for choice, and yet I hate the concept of abortion. ... I am pro-choice in every respect ... but I just hate it."
NBC News, October 24, 1999

"I am very, very proud to say that I'm pro-life."
Cleveland, Ohio, August 6, 2015

"I think the institution of marriage should be between a man and a woman."
The Advocate, February 15, 2000

"If two people dig each other, they dig each other."
Trump University Blog, December 22, 2005

"I'm against gay marriage."
Fox News, April 14, 2011

"It's like in golf. A lot of people—I don't want this to sound trivial—but a lot of people are switching to these really long putters, very unattractive. It's weird. You see these great players with these really long putters, because they can't sink three-footers anymore. And I hate it. I am a traditionalist. I have so many fabulous friends who happen to be gay, but I am a traditionalist."
New York Times, May 1, 2011

"It's always good to do things nice and complicated so that nobody can figure it out."
The New Yorker, May 19, 1997

"The simplest approach is often the most effective."
Trump: The Art of the Deal, 1987

"My attention span is short."
Trump: Surviving at the Top, 1990

"I have an attention span that's as long as it has to be."
Time, August 18, 2015

"I prefer to come to work each day and just see what develops."
Trump: The Art of the Deal, 1987

"You can't just sit around waiting for deals, opportunities, or a lucky break."
Trump: Think Big, 2007

"I look at things for the art sake and the beauty sake and for the deal sake."
New York magazine, July 11, 1988

"I'm just a fucking businessman."
Fortune, April 19, 2004

"I do listen to people. I hire experts. I hire top, top people. And I do listen."
Greenville, South Carolina, February 13, 2016

"I'm speaking with myself, No. 1, because I have a very good brain and I've said a lot of things. ... My primary consultant is myself."
MSNBC, March 16, 2016

"Don't think you're so smart that you can go it alone."
Trump: Surviving at the Top, 1990

"You must plan and execute your plan alone."
Think Like a Billionaire, 2004

"I couldn't be a one-man show …"
Trump: Surviving at the Top, 1990

"Think of yourself as a one-man army."
Trump: Think Like a Billionaire, 2004

"I like (and dislike) all sorts of people—winners, losers, and those in the middle!"
Trump: Think Like a Billionaire, 2004

"You'll find that when you become very successful, the people that you will like best are the people that are less successful than you, because when you go to a table you can tell them all of these wonderful

stories, and they'll sit back and listen. Does that make sense to you? Always be around unsuccessful people because everybody will respect you."
De Pere, Wisconsin, March 30, 2016

"I surround myself with good people, and then I give myself the luxury of trusting them."
Trump: Surviving at the Top, 1990

"My motto is 'Hire the best people, and don't trust them.'"
Trump: Think Big, 2007

"Surround yourself with people you can trust."
Trump: How to Get Rich, 2004

"People are too trusting. I'm a very untrusting guy."
Playboy, March 1990

"Expect the best from people."
Trump: Think Big, 2007

"The world is a vicious and brutal place. We think we're civilized. In truth, it's a cruel world and people are ruthless. They act nice to your face, but underneath they're out to kill you. ... Even your friends are out to get you: they want your job, they want your house, they want your money, they want your wife, and they even want your dog. Those are your friends; your enemies are even worse!"
Trump: Think Big, 2007

"If you have smart people working for you, they'll try to screw you if they think they can do better without you."
Daily Mail, October 30, 2010

"You know, I know the smart people. I really know the smart people. I deal with the smart people."
CNN, October 8, 1999

"You never want people to think you're a loser or a schlepper, but it's not a good idea if they think you're the smartest guy in the room, either."
Trump: Think Like a Billionaire, 2004

"I'm, like, a really smart person."
Phoenix Stump Speech, July 11, 2015

"You're generally better off sticking with what you know."
Trump: The Art of the Deal, 1987

"It's essential that you keep your mind open and alert."
Trump: Think Like a Billionaire, 2004

"All I know is what's on the Internet."
NBC News, March 13, 2016

"I see no value whatsoever in believing ignorance to be an attribute."
Trump: Think Like a Champion, 2009

"I love the poorly educated."
Las Vegas, February 23, 2016

"I've cultivated the learning habit over the years, and it's one of the most pleasurable aspects of my life."
> **Trump: How to Get Rich, 2004**

"Fortunately, I don't pride myself on being a know-it-all."
> **Trump: How to Get Rich, 2004**

"It would take an hour and a half to learn everything there is to learn about missiles. ... I think I know most of it anyway."
> **Washington Post, November 15, 1984**

"Small talk can be one of the best ways to educate yourself."
> **Trump: Think Like a Billionaire, 2004**

"I can't stand small talk."
> **Trump: The Art of the Deal, 1987**

"Stay as close to home as possible. Travel is time-consuming and, in my opinion, boring—especially compared with the fun I have doing deals in my office. I can never understand people who say that if they had a lot of money they would spend their time traveling. It's just not my thing."
   Trump: Surviving at the Top, 1990

"There's no excuse for staying home; the world's too fantastic to miss out on it. I wish I could travel more."
   Trump: Think Like a Billionaire, 2004

"Well, I read a lot … and over my life, I've read so much."
   The Hugh Hewitt Show, February 25, 2015

"I don't read much. Mostly I read contracts, but usually my lawyers do most of the work. There are too many pages."
   Veja, February 2014

"I don't have a lot of time for listening to television."
   New York Times, July 28, 2015

"I actually love watching television."
   The Hugh Hewitt Show, February 25, 2015

"I'm a thinker, and I have been a thinker. ... I'm a very deep thinker."
   Palm Beach, Florida, March 11, 2016

"The day I realized it can be smart to be shallow was, for me, a deep experience."
   Trump: Think Like a Billionaire, 2004

"I like it when people talk about me. As long as it is positive."
   LifeBeyondSport.com, undated

"I really value my reputation and I don't hesitate to sue."
   The Village Voice, January 15, 1979

> "I don't mind being criticized. I'll never, ever complain."
> **CNN, September 24, 2015**

ROFL…tears streaming….laughing…oh! cramps. My face hurts.

"When someone crosses you, my advice is 'Get even!' That is not typical advice, but it is real-life advice. If you do not get even, you are just a schmuck! When people wrong you, go after those people, because it is a good feeling and because other people will see you doing it. I love getting even. I get screwed all the time. I go after people, and you know what? People do not play around with me as much as they do with others. They know that if they do, they are in for a big fight. Always get even. Go after people that go after you. Don't let people push you around. Always fight back and always get even. It's a jungle out there, filled with bullies of all kinds who will try to push you around. If you're afraid to fight back people will think of you as a loser, a 'schmuck!' They will know they can get away with insulting you, disrespecting you, and taking advantage of you. Don't let it happen! Always fight back and get even."
Trump: Think Big, 2007

"If you can avoid an altercation, do so."
Trump: Think Like a Billionaire, 2004

"If someone attacks you, do not hesitate. Go for the jugular."
Trump: Think Big, 2007

"I don't want to be provocative, and in many cases I try not to be provocative."
Time to Get Tough: Making America #1 Again, 2011

"I do love provoking people. There is truth to that."
BuzzFeed, February 13, 2014

"Sometimes, part of making a deal is denigrating your competition."
Trump: The Art of the Deal, 1987

"If striving for wholeness means diminishing your competition, then your competition wasn't much to begin with."
Trump: Think Like a Champion, 2009

"Be tough, be smart, be personable, but don't take things personally."
Twitter, June 22, 2015

"It makes me feel so good to hit 'sleazebags' back."
Twitter, November 19, 2012

"You've gotta be nice."
The New Yorker, May 19, 1997
Baaa Ha Ha Ha!

"I do believe in hate when it's appropriate."
Trump: Surviving at the Top, 1990

"I think I am a nice person."
New York, June 16, 2015

Being on the other side of a relationship with someone like me must be difficult. "I'm no angel."
Rolling Stone, September 9, 2015

just being on the other side of the television screen from you is difficult enough.

"People who know me like me."
New York Stump Speech, June 16, 2015

"But there is nothing better than having a great marriage, in my opinion. There is nothing more beautiful, and there is nothing more important."
CNN, March 21, 2004

"You marry for love, but your signature on the marriage certificate is all about rights, duties, and property. It's a legally binding contract that knows nothing of love."
Trump: Think Big, 2007

"I've never been the kind of guy who takes his son out to Central Park to play catch, but I think I'm a good father."
Playboy, October 2004

"I like kids. I mean, I won't do anything to take care of 'em. I'll supply funds, and she'll take care of the kids."
The Howard Stern Show, April 2005

"I think I've been a very good husband."
CNN, February 9, 2011

"What the hell do I know, I've been divorced twice?"
Trump: Think Big, 2007

"Believe it or not, I'm a romantic guy."
Trump: Think Like a Billionaire, 2004

"Geraldo Rivera is a friend of mine, but he did something which I thought was absolutely terrible and he admits it was a mistake. He wrote a book naming many of the famous women that he slept with. I would never do that—I have too much respect for women in general, but if I did, the world would take serious notice. Beautiful, famous, successful, married—I've had them all, secretly, the world's biggest names, but unlike Geraldo I don't talk about it."
Trump: Think Big, 2007

"I don't have to brag. I don't have to. Believe it or not."
New York, June 16, 2015

"I avoid people with especially high opinions of their own abilities or worth."
Trump: Think Big, 2007

So, no mirrors for you…

"Hey, look, I went to the hardest school to get into, the best school in the world, I guess you could say, the Wharton School of Finance. It's like super genius stuff. I came out. I built a tremendous company. I had tremendous success. The Art of the Deal. The Apprentice. Everything."
CNN, August 11, 2015

"Do not look for approval from others. That is a sure sign of weakness."
Trump: Think Big, 2007

Gosh, I sure hope he likes this book!

"Look at my hands. … My hands are normal hands. During a debate, he was losing, and he said, 'Oh, he has small hands and therefore, you know what that means.' This was not me. This was Rubio that said, 'He has small hands and you know what that means.' OK? So, he started it. So, what I said a

couple of days later ... and what happened is, I was on line shaking hands with supporters, and one of the supporters got up and he said, 'Mr. Trump, you have strong hands. You have good-sized hands.' And then another one would say, 'You have great hands, Mr. Trump, I had no idea.' I said, 'What do you mean?' He said, 'I thought you were, like, deformed, and I thought you had small hands.' I had 50 people. ... I mean, people were writing, 'How are Mr. Trump's hands?' My hands are fine. You know, my hands are normal. Slightly large, actually. In fact, I buy a slightly smaller than large glove, OK?"
Washington Post, March 21, 2016

"Don't worry about actively promoting yourself."
Trump: Think Like a Billionaire, 2004

"Let people know what you've done. What good is it if no one knows about it? You've gotta be a promoter."
New York magazine, December 24, 1984

"Subtlety and modesty are appropriate for nuns and therapists."
Trump: How to Get Rich, 2004

"Everyone says, 'Oh, Trump is a great promoter.' I don't think I'm even a good promoter. If I get my name in the paper, if people pay attention, that's what matters. To me, that means it's a success."
Donald Trump: Master Apprentice, 2005

"Publicity gradually dehumanizes you."
Trump: Surviving at the Top, 1990

"I have learned that entertainment is a very simple business. You can be a horrible human being, you can be a truly terrible person, but if you get ratings, you are a king."
Time to Get Tough: Making America #1 Again, 2011

"It's fame itself that bends people out of shape. In fact, the more celebrities I meet, the more I realize that fame is a kind of drug, one that is way too powerful for most people to handle."
Trump: Surviving at the Top, 1990

"Everybody kisses your ass when you're hot. If you're not hot, they don't even call. So it's always good to stay hot."
CNBC, June 24, 2012

"I hate people that think they're hot stuff, and they're nothing."
Warren, Michigan, March 4, 2016

"I'm really concerned with the whole earthquake situation in L.A. I am a tremendous believer that someday Las Vegas may be the West Coast. … People in general are having lingering doubts about the value of real estate in L.A. It's happening too much and too often, the tremors. It's a very scary thing."
Los Angeles Times, July 24, 1988

"L.A. is going to be very hot, and it is very hot. The fact that Trump goes there makes it even hotter."
New York Times, February 5, 1990

"Anyone who thinks he's going to win them all is going to wind up a big loser."
Trump: Surviving at the Top, 1990

"I win, I win, I always win. In the end I always win, whether it's in golf, whether it's in tennis, whether it's in life, I just always win. And I tell people I always win, because I do."
Tim O'Brien's TrumpNation, 2005

"I do whine, because I want to win, and I'm not happy about not winning, and I am a whiner, and I keep whining and whining until I win."
CNN, August 11, 2015

"Toughness is knowing how to be a gracious winner—and rebounding quickly when you lose."
Trump: Surviving at the Top, 1990

"I don't like to lose."
New York Times, August 7, 1983

"I want to make America great again, and you can't do that if you come in a close second."
Washington Post, October 7, 2015

"We finished second, and I want to tell you something: I'm just honored. I'm really honored."
West Des Moines, Iowa, February 1, 2016

"Remember that in the best negotiations, everyone wins."
Trump: Never Give Up, 2008

"You hear lots of people say that a great deal is when both sides win. That is a bunch of crap."
Trump: Think Big, 2007

"I learned from my father that work can make you happy."
Trump: Think Big, 2007

"I think of it almost as a controlled neurosis, which is a quality I've noticed in many highly successful entrepreneurs. They're obsessive, they're driven, they're single-minded and sometimes they're almost maniacal, but it's all channeled into their work. … I don't say this trait leads to a happier life, or a better life, but it's great when it comes to getting what you want."
Trump: The Art of the Deal, 1987

"When you shake somebody's hand, go with it. It is very important. Shaking hands with someone means you are making a deal."
    Trump: Think Big, 2007

"Some business executives believe in a firm handshake. I believe in no handshake. It is a terrible practice. So often, I see someone who is obviously sick, with a bad cold or the flu, who approaches me and says, 'Mr. Trump, I would like to shake your hand.' It's a medical fact that this is how germs are spread."
    Trump: How to Get Rich, 2004

"You've got to take care of your body and stay healthy."
    Men's Health, March 3, 2013

"All my friends who work out all the time, they're going for knee replacements, hip replacements—they're a disaster."
New York Times Magazine, September 29, 2015

"Dress the part and act the part. Do not cause any doubt in anybody's mind that you don't know your stuff. When I moved to Manhattan to do my first deal, I did not have money or employees. When I went into an office, I acted as if I had an organization, The Trump Organization, behind me. I was on my own and no longer working for my father. Few people knew that The Trump Organization had no employees except myself and operated out of my studio apartment in Manhattan."
Trump: Think Big, 2007

"Sometimes people will come into my office and they will be great. They will look great, they'll sound great, they dress beautifully; everything is great. Then after you hire them they turn out to be morons. Sometimes a real slob will come in looking for a job. He does not dress well. He does not look good. He does not seem to be very smart. It turns out when you hire him or her, you find out you have hired a genius."
Trump: Think Big, 2007

"I do something wrong—I do things wrong—and when I do, I don't mind."
CNN, September 24, 2015

"It's amazing how often I am right."
Twitter, March 24, 2016

"You can't con people, at least not for long. You can create excitement, you can do wonderful promotion and get all kinds of press, and you can throw in a little hyperbole. But if you don't deliver the goods, people will eventually catch on. I think of Jimmy Carter. After he lost the election to Ronald Reagan, Carter came to see me in my office. He told me he was seeking contributions to the Jimmy Carter Library. I asked how much he had in mind. And he said, 'Donald, I would be very appreciative if you contributed five million dollars.' I was dumbfounded. I didn't even answer him. But that experience also taught me something. Until then, I'd never understood how Jimmy Carter became president. The answer is that as poorly qualified as he was for the job, Jimmy Carter had the nerve, the guts, the balls, to ask for something extraordinary. That ability above all helped him get elected president."
Trump: The Art of the Deal, 1987

" Jimmy Carter ... . He is a very nice man, but he wasn't my kind of president. I was more into the Ronald Reagans of the world. Nevertheless, after President Carter's term as President was up, he asked to meet me and of course I agreed. I didn't

know what he wanted in that I had never supported him and was actually very vocal on how poorly he handled our captives in Iran. ... Nevertheless, we had a wonderful conversation prior to getting to his point, which was, would I consider making a $50 million contribution to the Jimmy Carter Library? Here was a man that I had not supported, had not voted for, and yet he was in my office asking for a $50 million contribution! I said to myself, and I told the story many times, that Jimmy Carter, despite his image to the contrary, had an ability to think big. That's why he ran for President and others did not."
Trump: Think Big, 2007

"Ronald Reagan ... is so smooth and so effective a performer that he completely won over the American people. Only now, nearly seven years later, are people beginning to question whether there's anything beneath that smile."
Trump: The Art of the Deal, 1987

"... Ronald Reagan, to me, was a great president. And whether you are liberal or you're conservative, people really view him as a great president. He'll go down as a great president and not so much for the things he did, it's just, there was a demeanour to him and a spirit that the country had under Ronald Reagan that was really phenomenal. And, you

know, there was just a style and a class ... I mean, that's a really big part of being president. Ronald Reagan had it."
CNN, October 8, 1999

George H.W. Bush is "a great man. He's a man I support."
Washington Post, April 21, 1988

"But I disagree with him when he talks of a kinder, gentler America. I think if this country gets any kinder or gentler, it's literally going to cease to exist."
Playboy, March 1990

George W. Bush? "I like him."
CNN, October 8, 1999

"Don't talk to me about Bush, I was never a defender or a fan!"
Twitter, April 12, 2013

"I like John McCain."
Twitter, May 28, 2013

"I'm not a fan of John McCain."
Facebook, July 18, 2015

"Ron Paul has some serious ideas which deserve serious consideration. Wrong for media to ignore him."
Twitter, August 23, 2011

"He [Ron Paul] should be ignored."
Twitter, January 4, 2012

"[Mitt Romney] is the steady conservative who can restore America's future."
Twitter, February 22, 2012

"He's [Mitt Romney] a jealous fool and not a bright person. He's good looking. Other than that, he's got nothing."
New York Times, March 18, 2016

George Pataki is "the most underrated guy in American politics."
    Trump: The America We Deserve, 2000

Pataki "couldn't be elected dog catcher."
    Twitter, July 1, 2015

"Jeb Bush is a good man. I've held fundraisers for him. He's exactly the kind of political leader this country needs now and will very much need in the future. He, too, knows how to hang in there. His first shot at Florida's governorship didn't work out, but he didn't give up. He was campaigning the day after his loss. He won the next race in a landslide. He's bright, tough, and principled."
    Trump: The America We Deserve, 2000

"He's like a lost soul, Jeb Bush … this poor, pathetic, low-energy guy."
    Las Vegas, January 21, 2016

Barack Obama is "a strong guy who really knows what he wants."
    Fox News, February 9, 2009

"He's been a horrible president."
Fox News, April 14, 2011

"Here's a man that not only got elected, I think he's doing a really good job."
CNN, April 15, 2009

"Barack Obama has been the worst president ever."
Fox News, April 14, 2011

"Barack Obama is not who you think he is."
Twitter, October 15, 2012

"Oh, yes, he's a champion. I mean, he won against all odds. If you would have looked—when he first announced, people were giving him initially no chance. And he's just done something that's amazing. He's totally a champion."
CNN, April 15, 2009

"Hillary Clinton is definitely smart and resilient."
Trump: The America We Deserve, 2000

"Incompetent Hillary doesn't know what she's talking about. She doesn't have a clue. She's made such bad decisions."
      Fox News, March 22, 2016

"I think that a lot of people will be looking at Hillary's record as secretary of state, and she will be defending that, and I'm sure she'll do a good job of defending it."
      NBC News, August 10, 2013

"She was the worst secretary of state in the history of our nation. There's never been a secretary of state so bad as Hillary."
      NBC News, July 8, 2015

"I know Hillary and I think she'd make a great president …"
      Trump University Blog, March 13, 2008

"Hillary will be a disaster as a president."
      NBC News, July 9, 2015

"She has a husband that I also like very much."
CNN, September 24, 2007

"She's married to an abuser."
NBC News, January 10, 2016

President Trump? "He would believe very strongly in extreme military strength. He wouldn't trust anyone. He wouldn't trust the Russians."
Playboy, March 1990

"I have always felt that Russia and the United States should be able to work well with each other."
Reuters, December 18, 2015

"I see NATO as a good thing."
Washington Post, March 21, 2016

"I think NATO is obsolete."
ABC News, March 27, 2016

In favor of invading Iraq? "Yeah, I guess so."
   The Howard Stern Show, September 11, 2002

"It looks like a tremendous success from a military standpoint."
   Fox Business, March 21, 2003

"The war's a mess."
   Washington Post, March 25, 2003

"Qadhafi in Libya is killing thousands of people, nobody knows how bad it is, and we're sitting around, we have soldiers, all over the Middle East, and we're not bringing 'em in to stop this horrible carnage. ... We should go in, we should stop this guy, which would be very easy and very quick."
   Trump video blog, February 2011

"I never discussed that subject. I was in favor of Libya? We would be so much better off if Qadhafi were in charge right now."
   Houston, February 25, 2016

"Angela Merkel is doing a fantastic job ... Youth unemployment is at a record low and she has a budget surplus."
Twitter, October 3, 2013

She's [Angela Merkel] "ruining Germany."
Twitter, December 9, 2015

"Compromise is not a dirty word."
Manchester, NH, October 12, 2015

"I'm not big on compromise. I understand compromise. Sometimes compromise is the right answer, but oftentimes compromise is the equivalent of defeat, and I don't like being defeated."
Life, January 1989

"I'm walking, talking proof of the American Dream. For me, the American Dream is not just a dream; it's a reality."
Trump: Think Like a Billionaire, 2004

"The American Dream is dead."
New York, June 16, 2015

"Maybe we Americans pump ourselves up too much."
Trump: The America We Deserve, 2000

"We are the greatest country the world has ever known."
Time to Get Tough: Make America #1 Again, 2011

"I'm never self-satisfied."
Playboy, March 1990

"In truth I am dazzled as much by my own creations as are the tourists and glamour hounds that flock to Trump Tower."
Trump: Think Big, 2007

"If I were satisfied, I would not be Donald Trump."
Trump: Think Big, 2007

"I think there are two Donald Trumps."
Palm Beach, Florida, March 11, 2016

"I don't think there are two Donald Trumps. I think there's one Donald Trump."
Palm Beach, Florida, March 11, 2016

"Stop the indecisive internal dialogue before it starts. That is your biggest enemy."
Trump: Think Big, 2007

"I think we've had enough debates."
Fox News, March 16, 2016

"More debate is always better."
Twitter, December 7, 2011

"I mean, my whole life is a debate, but I don't debate."
South Bend, Indiana, May 2, 2016

"Sometimes—not often, but sometimes—less is more."
Trump: The Art of the Deal, 1987

"I always say, 'More is more.'"
Trump: Think Like a Billionaire, 2004

"New York is a great place. It's got great people. It's got loving people, wonderful people."
North Charleston, SC, January 14, 2016

"I know this city. There are some terrible people in this city."
Trump: Think Big, 2007

"Nobody owns me."
New York Post, April 18, 1999

"I'm owned by the people!"
Rolling Stone, September 9, 2015

"There's not a team."
MSNBC, March 8, 2016

"Yes, there is a team. I'm going to be forming a team."
MSNBC, March 8, 2016

"Eminent domain is wonderful."
Fox News, October 6, 2015

"I don't like eminent domain."
Breitbart News, November 5, 2015

"If you see somebody getting ready to throw a tomato, knock the crap out of 'em, would you? Seriously. OK? Just knock the hell—I promise you, I will pay the legal fees, I promise, I promise."
Cedar Rapids, Iowa, February 1, 2016

"I do not condone violence in any shape."
NBC News, March 13, 2016

"I believe in positive thinking, but I also believe in the power of negative thinking."
Playboy, March 1990

"I never think of the negative."
New York Times, August 7, 1983

"I always go into the deal anticipating the worst."
Trump: The Art of the Deal, 1987

"I believe in the power of positive thinking, but I never like to talk about it."
Washington Post, October 7, 2015

"I don't think positively, I don't think negatively."
Donald Trump: Master Apprentice, 2005

"I don't worry about anything."
New York Times Magazine, September 29, 2015

"I'm an environmentalist."
CNN, April 28, 2010

"Global warming is a total, and very expensive, hoax!"
Twitter, December 6, 2013

"I generally oppose gun control, but I support the ban on assault weapons and I support a slightly longer waiting period to purchase a gun."
Trump: The America We Deserve, 2000

"I am the strongest person running in favor of the Second Amendment."
Hanahan, South Carolina, February 15, 2016

"My sons love to hunt. They are members of the NRA, very proudly. I am a big believer in the Second Amendment."
Ayrshire, Scotland, July 31, 2015

"I'm not a hunter and don't approve of killing animals. I strongly disagree with my sons who are hunters."
Twitter, March 15, 2012

"[For a woman who has an abortion], there has to be some form of punishment."
MSNBC, March 30, 2016

"If Congress were to pass legislation making abortion illegal and the federal courts upheld this legislation, or any state were permitted to ban abortion under state and federal law, the doctor or any other person performing this illegal act upon a woman would be held legally responsible, not the woman …"
DonaldJTrump.com, March 30, 2016

"Millions and millions of women—cervical cancer, breast cancer—are helped by Planned Parenthood. So you can say whatever you want, but they have millions of women going through Planned Parenthood that are helped greatly."
Houston, February 25, 2016

"But Planned Parenthood should absolutely be defunded. I mean, if you look at what's going on with that, it's terrible."
Fox News, October 18, 2015

"I continue to alienate members of the press on occasion, but on the whole, I like them."
Trump: Think Like a Billionaire, 2004

"They are the most dishonest people in the world. The media. They are the worst. They are very dishonest people. They are terrible."
Indianapolis, April 20, 2016

"OK, no, I don't hate anybody. I love the media. They're wonderful."
Indianapolis, April 20, 2016

"I guess we wouldn't be here, maybe, if it wasn't for the media, so maybe we shouldn't be complaining."
Indianapolis, April 20, 2016

"Define yourself in a big way. We all have self-definitions; give yourself a big definition."
> **Trump: Think Big, 2007**

"You are what you think you are."
> **Trump: Think Big, 2007**

"I'm Swedish."
> **New York Times, November 1, 1976**

"I'm proud to have that German blood. Great stuff."
> **Kings of Kallstadt, 2014**

"I'm not the world's happiest person."
> **New York magazine, March 5, 1990**

"I'm a very happy man."
> **Forbes, October 1, 2009**

"The worst hell you will ever face is the hell you create with your own mind."
Trump: Think Big, 2007

"I'm very capable of changing to anything I want to change to."
Fox News, February 11, 2016

"I am me."
New York, April 26, 2016

"If you equivocate, it's an indication that you're unsure of yourself and what you're doing. It's also what politicians do all the time, and I find it inappropriate, insulting and condescending. I try not to do it."
Trump: How to Get Rich, 2004

TRUMP
Campaigner-in-Chief

"I've had a beautiful, I've had a flawless campaign. You'll be writing books about this campaign."

"I have no intention of running for President."
TIME, September 14, 1987

"I enjoy it, I enjoy the system. I doubt I'll ever be involved with politics beyond what I do right now, but I do enjoy the system. I find it, a really, really beautiful thing to watch."
CNN, 1988

"I would hate to think that people blame me for the problems of the world. Yet people come to me and say, 'Why do you allow homelessness in the cities?' as if I control the situation. I am not somebody seeking office."
Playboy, March 1990

"I don't want to be President. I'm 100 percent sure. I'd change my mind only if I saw this country continue to go down the tubes."
Playboy, March 1990

"I see the values of this country in the way crime is tolerated, where the people are virtually afraid to say, 'I want the death penalty.' Well, I want it. Where has this country gone when you're not supposed to put in a grave the son of a bitch who robbed, beat, murdered and threw a 90-year-old woman off the building?"
Playboy, March 1990

"I know politicians who love women who don't even want to be known for that, because they might lose the gay vote, OK?"
Playboy, March 1990

"Power corrupts."
Playboy, March 1990

"If I ever ran for office, I'd do better as a Democrat than as a Republican—and that's not because I'd be more liberal, because I'm conservative. But the working guy would elect me. He likes me. When I walk down the street, those cabbies start yelling out their windows."
Playboy, 1990

"I don't want the Presidency. I'm going to help a lot of people with my foundation—and for me, the grass isn't always greener."
Playboy, 1990

"I love Oprah. Oprah would always be my first choice [for Vice President]"

"She's popular, she's brilliant, she's a wonderful woman," Trump said of the talk show queen. "I mean, if she'd ever do it. I don't know that she'd ever do it."
Larry King Live, October 8, 1999

> A new study claims the stress of being president takes three years off your life. So suddenly everyone is thinking of voting for Trump."
> **—Conan O'Brien**

"Perhaps I shouldn't campaign at all, I'll just, you know, I'll ride it right into the White House."
Larry King Live, 1999

"My entire life, I've watched politicians bragging about how poor they are, how they came from nothing, how poor their parents and grandparents were. And I said to myself, if they can stay so poor for so many generations, maybe this isn't the kind of person we want to be electing to higher office. How smart can they be? They're morons."
New York Times with Maureen Dowd, November 28, 1999

"I think I'm like the largest or one of the largest [political] contributors. I'm maxed out every year."
Larry King Live, October 8, 1999

In 1999, Donald Trump was considering a run for White House, he proposed a one-time 14.25% tax on those with a net worth of over $10 million, which would equal $5.7 trillion, wiping away the national debt.

The headline on Nov. 10, 1999 read:
"Soak the Rich."

"I give him a lot of credit. I think he'll go down -- his legacy, really, will be the Reform Party much more so than, you know, we make money; he makes money, I make money, we make a lot of money. But the legacy that he's created, the Reform Party, is a great tribute to him, and I think he'll go down, and I think he'll be given great credit for it."
Larry King Live, October 8, 1999

On Ross Perot "going down"

"One of the key problems today is that politics is such a disgrace. Good people don't go into government. I'd want to change that."
The Advocate, February 15, 2000

"It's very possible that I could be the first presidential candidate to run and make money on it."
Fortune, April 3, 2000

Donald Trump paid nearly $12.5 million to his own businesses and family members during his 18-month campaign for president, a CNN review of federal reports shows.
CNN Money, December 2016

"40 Wall Street actually was the second-tallest building in downtown Manhattan... And now it's the tallest."
WWOR/UPN 9 News New York. Sept. 11, 2001

Donald Trump, bragging about his building following the 9/11 attack. 70 Pine Street, just a block away, is actually bigger.

"I think of myself as a young guy, but I'm not so young anymore. And I've been around for a long time. And it just seems that the economy does better under the Democrats than the Republicans."
Late Edition with Wolf Blitzer, 2004

KING: By the way, before we take the next call, you considered, once, running for the presidency.

TRUMP: Well, I didn't consider it long. I had a group. They did a poll and the poll came — I did a favour for a trend friend of mine in New Hampshire. He went to the Wharton School of Finance. He said, Donald, would you come up and make a speech to a business group. I came up to New Hampshire as a favour to him. I made a speech.

And everyone thought I was running for president.

KING: You didn't say I am not.

TRUMP: No I kept it going for about two weeks. But I wasn't running. I love what I'm doing.

KING: You think it will be a close election?

TRUMP: I think it's going to be very close. I think it's going to be John Kerry against Bush. I know them both. They're both good guys and I think will be a close race.
Larry King Live, August 08, 2004

"Condoleezza Rice, she's a lovely woman, but I think she's a bitch. She goes around to other countries and other nations, negotiates with their leaders, comes back and nothing ever happens."
Learning Annex Real Estate & Wealth Expo, November 19, 2006

Condoleeza replied via Facebook:
"I can't wait until November 9!"

"Look at the trouble Bill Clinton got into with something that was totally unimportant and they tried to impeach him, which was nonsense. And yet Bush got us into this horrible war with lies, by lying, by saying they had weapons of mass destruction, by saying all sorts of things that turned out not to be true."

CNN Newsroom , October 15, 2008

"Hillary is smart, tough and a very nice person, and so is her husband. Bill Clinton was a great President. They are fine people. Hillary was roughed up by the media, and it was a tough campaign for her, but she's a great trooper. Her history is far from being over."

Trump University Blog, 2008

"Frankly, had he not met Monica, had he not met Paula, had he not met various and sundry semi-beautiful women, he would have had a much better deal going."

Morning Joe, 2008

Trump said Bill Clinton was his favourite president of the last four

"Our leaders are stupid. They are stupid people. It's just very, very sad."
Las Vegas, April 28, 2011

"When you need zone changes, you're political. … You know, I'll support the Democrats, the Republicans, whatever the hell I have to support."
BuzzFeed, Feb. 13, 2014

"@AlexSalmond, Wind turbines are ripping your country apart and killing tourism.Electric bills in Scotland are skyrocketing-stop the madness"
Twitter, March 19, 2014

"Obama is, without question, the WORST EVER president. I predict he will now do something really bad and totally stupid to show manhood!"
Twitter, June 5, 2014

Its been almost a month, will I ever get used to Trump? Fuck no. Its like watching a toddler playing with a gun - you're always nervous.
— **Bill Maher**

"The U.S. cannot allow EBOLA infected people back. People that go to far away places to help out are great-but must suffer the consequences!"
Twitter, August 1, 2014

Suffering the consequences of compassion

"Republican pollster Frank Luntz is a "total loser!"
Twitter, Aug. 3, 2014

"If Obama resigns from office NOW, thereby doing a great service to the country—I will give him free lifetime golf at any one of my courses!"
Twitter, September 10, 2014

"But what I don't do is, I don't tweet about people who've insulted me. I try to sleep so that in the morning I'm actually ready for crises," Obama said, referring to the prolific tweets from Trump, often late at night.

"President Obama - close down the flights from Ebola infected areas right now, before it is too late! What the hell is wrong with you?"
Twitter, October 4, 2014

"I have a big plane. He doesn't."
Des Moines Register, April 8, 2015

Well sure, but his penis is probably adult-size

"I have lost a lot during this Presidential run defending the people of the United States. I have always heard that it is very hard for a successful person to run for President. Macy's, NBC, Serta and NASCAR have all taken the weak and very sad position of being politically correct even though they are wrong in terms of what is good for our country,"

Freedom Summit in Greenville, South Carolina May 9, 2015

"I will be the greatest jobs president God ever created."
Trump Tower, June 16, 2015

Aha! On the eighth day, God created jobs presidents...

"Romney — I have a Gucci store that's worth more than Romney."
Des Moines Register, June 2015

This is, in fact true....but, it' still a douchey thing to say.

"I'm using my own money. I'm not using lobbyists. I'm not using donors. I don't care. I'm really rich."
Trump Tower, June 16, 2015

The largest source of Trump funds is small donors giving under $200. In total, these small donors have given $45.2 million...
The Huffington Post October 11, 2016

"We have a disaster called the big lie: Obamacare ... And it's going to get worse, because remember, Obamacare really kicks in in '16, 2016. Obama is going to be out playing golf."
Campaign Announcement, June 15, 2015

Was it all a hoax?

In June 2015, the New York Daily News featured Trump on the cover with the headline "You're Hired!" Reportedly, Trump paid actors $50 to appear in the audience during his speech where he announced his run for the presidency. The claim came from a story by the Hollywood Reporter that uncovered an email seeking background actors for the event.

"NBC is weak, and like everybody else is trying to be politically correct— that is why our country is in serious trouble"
June 29, 2015

Trump statement following NBCUniversal's severing of their relationship.

"Rick Perry, I don't think even understands what he is saying."

The Atlantic, July 2015

"Rick Perry put on glasses so people think he's smart. … People can see through the glasses."

Bluffton SC, July 21, 2015

"The hatred that clown @krauthammer has for me is unbelievable – causes him to lie when many others say Trump easily won debate."

Twitter, August 7, 2015

The record ratings for the Republican debate earlier this month? "Who do you think they're watching? Jeb Bush? Huh? I don't think so."

Birch Run, Mich., August. 11, 2015

"Donald Trump is the kind of person who goes to the Super Bowl and thinks the people in the huddle are talking about him."

—Eric Schneiderman

340

"Truly weird Senator Rand Paul of Kentucky reminds me of a spoiled brat without a properly functioning brain."
Twitter, Aug. 10, 2015

"My plan will lower taxes for our country, not raise them. Phony @club4growth says I will raise taxes —just another lie."
Twitter, September 15, 2015

True, but middle income earners will only see 0.8 percent benefit, while the top 1 percent earners will get to pay an average of 14.5 percent less in taxes.

"An analysis of the plan by the Urban-Brookings Tax Policy Center found that the Trump plan was disproportionately beneficial to the wealthy, and would greatly increase the national debt. "
The Fiscal Times

"Lightweight Senator @RandPaul should focus on trying to get elected in Kentucky--- a great state which is embarrassed by him."
Twitter, September 12, 2015

"I will tell you that our system is broken. I gave to many people. Before this, before two months ago, I was a businessman. I give to everybody. When they call, I give. And do you know what? When I need something from them two years later, three years later, I call them—they are there for me."
Republican Presidential Debate
August 6, 2015

Explaining how he's part of the problem...

"I just realized that if you listen to Carly Fiorina for more than ten minutes straight, you develop a massive headache. She has zero chance!"
Twitter, August 9, 2015

> "It's like an Internet comment troll ran for president."
>
> —Jon Stewart

"Huma Abedin, the top aide to Hillary Clinton and the wife of perv sleazebag Anthony Wiener, was a major security risk as a collector of info"
Twitter, August 31 2015 ·

"The line of 'Make America Great Again,' the phrase, that was mine, I came up with it about a year ago, and I kept using it, and everybody's using it, they are all loving it. I don't know; I guess I should copyright it, maybe I have copyrighted it."
My Fox New York, March 2015

President Ronald Reagan coined the slogan during his campaign more than three decades ago.

During the CNN GOP debate, moderator Jake Tapper asked Dr. Ben Carson if he believes that vaccines can cause autism. He does not. When the question was asked of Donald Trump, however, he responded:

"I am totally in favour of vaccines. But I want smaller doses over a longer period of time. Same exact amount, but you take this little beautiful baby, and you pump--I mean, it looks just like it's meant for a horse, not for a child, and we've had so many instances, people that work for me. ... [in which] a child, a beautiful child went to have the vaccine, and came back and a week later had a tremendous fever, got very, very sick, now is autistic."
September 2015

"Now, the poor guy — you've got to see this guy, 'Ah, I don't know what I said! I don't remember!'"
Campaign Rally, November 26, 2015

Donald Trump, mocking New York Times investigative reporter Serge Kovaleski, by jerking his arms in front of his body. Kovaleski has a physical disability called arthrogryposis that limits flexibility in his arms.

"I spend millions a year, or millions of dollars on ramps, and get rid of the stairs and different kinds of elevators all over and I'm gonna mock? I would never do that," he continued.

"Number one, I have a good heart. Number two, I'm a smart person."

"I've seen numbers of 24 percent — I actually saw a number of 42 percent unemployment. Forty-two percent. 5.3 percent unemployment -- that is the biggest joke there is in this country. ... The unemployment rate is probably 20 percent, but I will tell you, you have some great economists that will tell you it's a 30, 32. And the highest I've heard so far is 42 percent."
September 28, 2015

According to the U.S. Bureau of Labor Statistics, the unemployment rate as 5.5%...no conspiracy theory...just statistics.

"How stupid are the people of Iowa?"
Ft. Dodge Iowa rally, 2015.

"It's really cold outside, they are calling it a major freeze, weeks ahead of normal. Man, we could use a big fat dose of global warming!"
Twitter, October 19, 2015,

"[Hillary Clinton] was gonna beat Obama. I don't know who would be worse, I don't know, how could it be worse? But she was going to beat – she was favored to win – and she got schlonged, she lost, I mean she lost."

Grand Rapids MI, December 21, 2015

"I like China. I just sold an apartment for $15 million to someone from China. Am I supposed to dislike them?"

GOP debate, January 28, 2016

"There may be somebody with tomatoes in the audience. If you see somebody getting ready to throw a tomato, knock the crap out of them, would you? Seriously. Okay? Just knock the hell -- I promise you, I will pay for the legal fees."

Cedar Rapids Iowa, February 1, 2016

"That was so great. Who was the person who did that? Put up your hand, put up your hand. Bring that person up here. I love that."

Praise for two audience members who tackled a protester

"A person who thinks only about building walls, wherever they may be, and not building bridges, is not Christian."

— **Pope Francis**

"For a religious leader to question a person's faith is disgraceful. I am proud to be a Christian. ... If and when the Vatican is attacked by ISIS, which as everyone knows is ISIS' ultimate trophy, I can promise you that the Pope would have only wished and prayed that Donald Trump would have been President because this would not have happened."
February 18, 2016

"I love the old days, you know? You know what I hate? There's a guy totally disruptive, throwing punches, we're not allowed punch back anymore. I'd like to punch him in the face, I'll tell ya."
Nevada, February 22, 2016

"At a rally in Las Vegas last night Donald Trump told supporters he'd like to punch protesters in the face. Though he looks more like the kind of guy who would stroke a white cat while somebody else punched you in the face."

—**Seth Meyers**

"One of the things I'm going to do if I win... I'm going to open up our libel laws so when they write purposely negative and horrible and false articles, we can sue them and win lots of money,"
    Fort Worth Texas, February 22, 2016

"We're going to open up those libel laws so when The New York Times writes a hit piece, which is a total disgrace, or when the Washington Post, which is there for other reasons, writes a hit piece, we can sue them and win money instead of having no chance of winning because they're totally protected," he said. "We're going to open up libel laws and we're going to have people sue you like you've never got sued before."
    Fort Worth Texas, February 22, 2016

"Listen to this. We won with everything. We won with women. I love the women. We won with women." (Cheers and applause)
We won with men. Meh, I'd rather win with women, to be honest, but that's all right. We won with evangelicals. Unbelievable. Unbelievable. We won with the military. (Cheers and applause) We won — oh, oh, oh. (...) We won with highly educated, pretty well educated and poorly educated, but we won

with everything. Tall people, short people, fat people, skinny people — just won. (Cheering) (...)
"The only category I do badly in is my personality, and that's OK. Who cares? And you know what? You want to know something? I'm a better person than the people I'm running against. I see it. Let me tell you."

Atlanta, February 22, 2016

"You know these politicians that I'm dealing with? I mean, they're up on the stage these people, they don't a clue...some are nice guys actually, some I don't like, some I do like and it's whatever — I won't get into the ones that left, because they're gone. You know, once they're gone, they're gone, right? They leave, they leave, good luck, we think you're wonderful. How do you like them? Wonderful people, they're great."

Atlanta, February 22, 2016

"You talk about George Bush, say what you want, the World Trade Center came down during his time. He was president, okay? Don't blame him or don't blame him, but he was president, the World Trade Center came down during his reign."

GOP Debate, February 2016

"We won with poorly educated. I love the poorly educated."
Nevada Caucus, February 23, 2016

"We're totally predictable. And predictable is bad. Sitting at a meeting like this and explaining my views and if I do become president, I have these views that are down for the other side to look at, you know. I hate being so open."
The Washington Post, March 2, 2016

"Why would anyone in Florida vote for lightweight Senator Marco Rubio. Check out his credit card scam, his house sale & his no show voting!"
Twitter, March 2, 2016

"Perhaps she made the story up. I think that's what happened."
To Reporters, March 10, 2016

On Breitbart reporter Michelle Fields, who accused Trump campaign manager Corey Lewandowski of grabbing her arm aggressively as she attempted to question the candidate. Fields tweeted a photo of her bruised arm, and news accounts corroborated her story.

"The press is now going, they're saying, 'Oh but there's such violence.' No violence. You know how many people have been hurt at our rallies? I think, like, basically none except maybe somebody got hit once. It's a love fest. These are love fests. And every once in a while ... somebody will stand up and they'll say something.... It's a little disruption, but there's no violence. There's none whatsoever."
March 14, 2016

"I think you'd have riots. I think you'd have riots. I'm representing many, many millions of people. In many cases first-time voters ... If you disenfranchise those people? And you say, well, I'm sorry, you're 100 votes short, even though the next one is 500 votes short? I think you'd have problems like you've never seen before. I wouldn't lead it, but I think bad things will happen."
CNN interview, March 16, 2016

On what will happen if he doesn't win the GOP nomination

"I'd work on spirit because the spirit is so low, it's incredible, the unemployment, you look at unemployment for black youth in this country, African American youth, is 58-59 percent. It's unthinkable. Unemployment for African Americans – not youth, but African Americans – is very high. And I would create in the inner cities, which is what I really do best, that's why when I open a building and I show you it's way ahead of schedule, under budget and everything else—I think it was the Rite Aid store, the store in Baltimore it took them 20 years to get it built, one store, and then it burned down in one night—we have to create incentives for people to love what they are doing, and to make money. And to create, you know, to really create a better life for themselves."

The Washington Post, March 21, 2016

"She had a pen in her hand, which Secret Service is not liking because they don't know what it is, whether it's a little bomb."

CNN town hall, March 29, 2016

On reporter Michelle Fields, who was assaulted by Trump's campaign manager, Corey Lewandowski, when she tried to ask Trump a question after a rally.

"She's not a baby. She was grabbing me. Am I supposed to press charges against her?"
CNN town hall, March 29, 2016

Suggesting it was Michelle Fields who was the aggressor...Lewandowski was arrested on battery charges (that were dropped) following the incident.

"I wrote this out, and it's very close to my heart. Because I was down there and I watched our police and our firemen down at 7/11, down at the World Trade Center right after it came down. And I saw the greatest people I've ever seen in action."
Buffalo, New York, April 18, 2016

"I don't think I'm going to lose, but if I do, I don't think you're ever going to see me again, folks. I think I'll go to Turnberry and play golf or something."
Maryland, April 24, 2016

"I think the only card she has is the women's card. She has got nothing else going. Frankly, if Hillary Clinton were a man, I don't think she would get 5% of the vote. And the beautiful thing is women don't like her, ok?"
**Victory press conference,
New York, April 26, 2016**

"His father was with Lee Harvey Oswald prior to Oswald's being – you know, shot. I mean, the whole thing is ridiculous. What is this, right prior to his being shot, and nobody even brings it up. They don't even talk about that. That was reported, and nobody talks about it."
Trump later added, "I mean what was he doing with Lee Harvey Oswald, shortly before the death – before the shooting? It's horrible."
Fox and Friends, May 3, 2016

Donald Trump, suggesting that Ted Cruz's father may have been involved in the assassination of President John F. Kennedy, despite the fact that no proof exists of any such link. To be fair, he got the info from The National Enquirer — whom he stated was a publication worthy of the Pulitzer Prize....no, seriously.

"From a moral standpoint, I believe in it. But you also have to get elected. And there's no way a Republican is going to beat a Democrat when the Republican is saying, 'We're going to cut your Social Security' and the Democrat is saying, 'We're going to keep it and give you more."
**Bloomberg Businessweek,
May 26, 2016**

Donald Trump, privately explaining to House Speaker Paul Ryan that he has a "public and private position" on Social Security.

"We're gonna bring businesses back. We're gonna have businesses that used to be in New Hampshire, that are now in Mexico, come back to New Hampshire, and you can tell them to go f**k themselves. Because they let you down, and they left!"
Portsmouth, New Hampshire May 2016

"Crooked Hillary is wheeling out one of the least productive senators in the U.S. Senate, goofy Elizabeth Warren, who lied on heritage."
Twitter, June 27, 2016

"I don't care. It's a long time ago. And he voted that way and they were also misled. A lot of information was given to people…"
60 Minutes, July 17, 2016

Forgiving his running mate, Mike Pence, for voting in favour of the Iraq war, saying he was "entitled to make a make mistake," but adding that Hillary Clinton isn't.

"I alone can fix it."
Republican National Convention, July 21, 2016

Trump on America

"I don't know what hotel this is, but you ought to try turning on the air conditioning or we're not going to get you paid."
Roanoke, July 26, 2016

Ranting about a hot ballroom. The hotel said the air conditioning system was working properly

"You know what I wanted to. I wanted to hit a couple of those speakers so hard. I would have hit them. No, no. I was going to hit them, I was all set and then I got a call from a highly respected governor... I was gonna hit one guy in particular, a very little guy. I was gonna hit this guy so hard his head would spin and he wouldn't know what the hell happened... I was going to hit a number of those speakers so hard their heads would spin, they'd never recover. And that's what I did with a lot – that's why I still don't have certain people endorsing me: they still haven't recovered."
Iowa, July 29, 2016

Emotionally mature reaction to the DNC speakers.

"I think I've made a lot of sacrifices. I work very, very hard. I've created thousands and thousands of jobs, tens of thousands of jobs, built great structures. I've had tremendous success. I think I've done a lot."
ABC News, July 30, 2016

Rejecting the assertion by Muslim lawyer Khizr Khan, whose son died in Iraq in 2004, that Trump had "sacrificed nothing and no one." Trump was unable to name an actual sacrifice when pressed to elaborate.

"Look at his wife, she was standing there. She had nothing to say. She probably, maybe she wasn't allowed to have anything to say. You tell me."

"I'd like to hear his wife say something."
ABC News, July 30, 2016

Implying that Ghazala Khan, the mother of a fallen American soldier, was not allowed to speak due to her religion.

"We do, if it's illegals, in other words, if it's everybody, but people that are legally living here, I'm doing very well. In other words, people that are here, like Hispanics that are in the country, I'm doing very well. People that vote. Like people leaving voting booths and all, I'm doing very well with them."
The Washington Post, 2016

Yesterday, Donald Trump Tweeted angrily that millions of people voted illegally on election day. Then someone told Trump it's not illegal for women to vote.

— **Conan O'Brien**

"They don't write good. They have people over there, like Maggie Haberman and others, they don't — they don't write good. They don't know how to write good."
Fox News with Sean Hannity, Aug. 1, 2016

NY Times rant becomes a grammatical clusterf#ck

"This business tax will also end job-killing corporate inversions and cause trillions in new dollars in wealth to come pouring into our country and, by the way, into titties like right here in Detroit."
August 8, 2016

"The Tax Foundation tells NPR that it estimates Trump's plan would add around 0.5 percentage points to economic growth each year."
— NPR
September 19, 2016

"If she gets to pick her judges – nothing you can do, folks. Although, the Second Amendment people. Maybe there is. I don't know."
Wilmington, NC, August 9, 2016

"For evangelicals, for the Christians, for the everybody, for everybody of religion, this will be, may be, the most important election that our country has ever had. And once I get in, I will do my thing that I do very well. And I figure it is probably, maybe the only way I'm going to get to heaven. So I better do a good job."
Speaking to evangelical leaders Orlando FL, August 11, 2016

"I might lie to you like Hillary does all the time, but I'll never lie to Giacomo, okay?"
Connecticut, August 13, 2016

Admitting to lying to voters while saying he would not lie to the 18-year-old cancer patient in the audience, Giacomo Brancado

"Dwyane Wade's (sic) cousin was just shot and killed walking her baby in Chicago. Just what I have been saying. African-Americans will VOTE TRUMP!"
Twitter, August 27, 2016

Even the tragic death of a woman he never met is all about him

"I think what we should do is — she goes around with armed bodyguards like you have never seen before. I think that her bodyguards should drop all weapons. They should disarm. Right? Right? I think they should disarm – immediately. What do you think? Yes? Yes. Yeah. Take their guns away! She doesn't want guns. Take their — let's see what happens to her."
On Hillary Clinton, September 16, 2016

"Big statement, fellas! You're not going to write it. That's huge. But they're letting people pour into the country so they can go and vote."
NBPS Roundtable, October 7, 2016

To vote, one must be a citizen born in the USA or naturalized, which takes about 5 years.

""For those who control the levers of power in Washington, and for the global special interests, they partner with these people that don't have your good in mind. Our campaign represents a true existential threat like they haven't seen before."
West Palm Beach, October 13, 2016

"This election will determine whether we are a free nation, or whether we have only the illusion of democracy, but are in fact controlled by a small handful of global special interests rigging the system. And our system is rigged. This is reality."
West Palm Beach, October 13, 2016

[Hillary Clinton] "the vessel (of) a corrupt global establishment that's raiding our country and surrendering the sovereignty of our nation."
West Palm Beach, October 13, 2016

"This is not simply another four-year election; This is a crossroads in the history of our civilization that will determine whether or not we, the people, reclaim control over our government. The political establishment that is trying to stop us is the same group responsible for our disastrous trade deals, massive illegal immigration, and economic and foreign policies that have bled our country dry."
West Palm Beach, October 13, 2016

So, I see they got him to use the teleprompter again....those words came out of his mouth, but they didn't come out of his brain.

"This election will determine whether we remain a free country in the truest sense of the word or we become a corrupt banana republic controlled by large donors and foreign governments. The election of Hillary Clinton would lead to the destruction of our country."
West Palm Beach, October 13, 2016

"Polls close, but can you believe I lost large numbers of women voters based on made up events THAT NEVER HAPPENED. Media rigging election!"
Twitter, October 16, 2016

"Watched Saturday Night Live hit job on me. Time to retire the boring and unfunny show. Alec Baldwin portrayal stinks. Media rigging election!"
Twitter, October 16, 2016

"Without the media, Hillary Clinton couldn't be elected dogcatcher," Trump told his Pennsylvania audience. For months he has claimed that the political system, along with national institutions that have gone unquestioned for decades–from the Bureau of Labor Statistics to the FBI–are rigged against him. That includes Republican leaders. "I wouldn't want to be in a foxhole with a lot of these people," he told Fox News' Bill O'Reilly on Oct. 11, "especially Ryan."

Time, October 24, 2016

During a rally this Wednesday in Lakeland, Fla., Trump talked about a woman who had fainted but returned to the crowd:
"The woman was out cold and now she's coming back. See? We don't go by these new, and very much softer, NFL rules. Concussion. Oh, oh! Got a little ding on the head. No, no, you can't play for the rest of the season. Our people are tough."

Lakeland FL, October 12, 2016

"I don't care how sick you are, I don't care if you just came back from the doctor and he gave you the worst possible prognosis, meaning it's over, you won't be around in two weeks. Doesn't matter. Hang out till Nov. 8. Get out and vote."

Trump then assured those dying people that after they are gone…

"all we're going to say is, 'We love you and we will remember you always.'"..."I say kiddingly, but I mean it."
Nevada Rally, October 5, 2016

"My Social Security contribution will go up, as will Donald's—assuming he can't find a way to get out of it," Clinton joked in response to a question about entitlement reform.

"Such a nasty woman," Trump said as he leaned into the microphone.
Final Debate, October 19, 2016

The Lady Donald Doth Protest Too Much

"I have much better judgment than she does. There's no question about that," Trump said as Clinton stood smiling on the Hofstra University debate stage.

"I also have a much better temperament than she has," Trump added. "I have a winning temperament. I know how to win. She does not have a winning temperament."

As the audience broke out in audible laughter, Trump powered through his attempt to associate the Democratic presidential nominee with one his greatest vulnerabilities by embracing it as an advantage for himself.

"I think my strongest asset, maybe by far, is my temperament. I have a winning temperament. I know how to win," Trump said.

"I think my single-greatest asset of any assets I have is my temperament, and I know how to win," Trump said at a North Carolina rally earlier this month. He repeated the line during an interview with ABC News that same day.

"A lot of people have said that that know me that maybe my greatest strength is my temperament," Trump told Fox News in August.

Even in the Feb. 6 GOP primary debate, Trump claimed, "I actually think I have the best temperament."

Sophia Tesfaye, salon.com
September 27, 2016

TRUMP
Tweeter-in-Chief

Many people have said I'm the world's greatest writer of 140 character sentences.

Every tappity-tap-tap of Donald Drumpf's infant-sized fingers, draws a roar from the virtual crowd. Eschewing traditional campaign advertising venues and traditional media buys, Trump harnessed the Internet in the 2016 election with admittedly spectacular success. He has turned Twitter into the loudest, largest, longest campaign rally in history.

With 17.4 million followers, every Drumpf Tweet garners thousands of retweets, replies, heated arguments and conversations every single day....all day... and it has been this way since around 2012/13.

In the beginning, around 2009, @realdonaldtrump mostly tweeted quotes from his books, until staffers introduced him to the possibilities. Apparently Trump likens his Twitter activity to having his own newspaper — and he's not wrong — plenty of newspapers would love to have a rabid, engaged list of subscribers over 17 million names long.

I like CNN and the New York Times, but I'm not frothing at the mouth over it. I read it. I keep articles occasionally. It is an enhancement to my knowledge and stimulation of my intellect and curiosity...I don't stand on street corners shouting about what I've read there. I don't engage perfect strangers in lengthy battles of wits and words over every little sentence. I don't issue death threats to my fellow readers. Trump's legions of vociferous followers do that in the virtual world every day…..and Trump is paying attention. Like money, he sees Twitter mentions and retweets as a way to keep score.

I couldn't, wouldn't and shouldn't share every one of Trump's Twitter utterances with you here. I provide just enough; You'll get the idea. Trump uses his Twitter account mostly to spread lies, praise himself and lob insults from afar. Trump is the worst kind of bully…..the chicken-shit kind. He says things that, given the opportunity, he would never say to someone's face. After insulting Carly Fiorina's face, he back-pedalled sheepishly when she confronted him about it at a GOP debate.

In 140 characters and less, Trump lets us glimpse his sad soul. Impulsive, ignorant, jealous and impetuous, like a small child Trump just can't seem to stop himself. He has no ability to self-regulate. His Twitter feed is unfiltered and unapologetic.

What strikes me most is how lonely he must be. What human being, who enjoys a full life and real relationships, spends his wee morning hours tweeting about Katy Perry's marriage or Kirsten Stewart's fidelity to her Twilight co-star Robert Pattinson?

I'd feel pity for him….if he wasn't such a dick.

"She better get the hell out. If she goes back, she's a loser, and she doesn't deserve to have any future success."
Twitter, March 9, 2009

A touching message to Rhianna after Chris Brown beat her.

I feel sorry for Rosie 's new partner in love whose parents are devastated at the thought of their daughter being with @Rosie--a true loser.
December 14, 2011

"Barney Frank looked disgusting--nipples protruding--in his blue shirt before Congress. Very very disrespectful."
December 21, 2011

"Govt. collapsing in Iraq only 2 weeks after withdrawal of our troops. Sadly, I called this one and please remember, I alone called it."
December 27, 2011

"Global warming has been proven to be a canard repeatedly over and over again. The left needs a dose of reality."
March 28, 2012

"The TIME Magazine cover showing late age breast feeding is disgusting--sad what TIME did to get noticed. @TIME"
May 14, 2012

"Cher is somewhat of a loser. She's lonely. She's unhappy. She's very miserable."
May 15, 2012

"Wind Farms are not only disgusting to look at but also cause tremendous damage to their local ecosystems."
June 28, 2012

"Ariana Huffington is unattractive, both inside and out. I fully understand why her former husband left her for a man. He made a good decision."
August 28, 2012

The Emmys were horrendous...the absolute worst show!
September 24, 2012

If The Apprentice won one however, he would have gushed that it was the most tremendous show in history....and the rating were YUGE!

"@katyperry is no bargain but I don't like John Mayer--he dates and tells--be careful Katy (just watch!)."
October 16, 2012

"@katyperry I watched Russell Brand and I think his mind is fried - he looks really bad. Russell is a total joke, a dummy who is lost!"
October 16, 2012

"@katyperry Katy, what the hell were you thinking when you married loser Russell Brand. There is a guy who has got nothing going, a waste!"
October 16, 2012

"@katyperry must have been drunk when she married Russell Brand @rustyrockets – but he did send me a really nice letter of apology!"
October 16, 2012

I could find no evidence of this letter of apology.

"@antbaxter Thanks for helping promote & make Trump International Golf Links Scotland so successful--you stupid fool!"
October 16, 2012

You're Welcome?

"Wind turbines are not only killing millions of birds, they are killing the finances & environment of many countries & communities."
Twitter, October 17, 2012

"Remember, new "environment friendly" lightbulbs can cause cancer. Be careful-- the idiots who came up with this stuff don't care."
Twitter, October 17, 2012

"Robert Pattinson should not take back Kristen Stewart. She cheated on him like a dog & will do it again--just watch. He can do much better!"
October 17, 2012

"Robert I'm getting a lot of heat for saying you should dump Kristen- but I'm right. If you saw the Miss Universe girls you would reconsider."
October 18, 2012

"So many tweets & stories on Stewart/Pattinson Look, it doesn't matter-- the relationship will never be the same. It is permanently broken."
October 19, 2012

From the man who cheated on both wife one and wife two…

"Everyone knows I am right that Robert Pattinson should dump Kristen Stewart. In a couple of years, he will thank me. Be smart, Robert."
October 22, 2012

"Everyone is asking me to speak more on Robert & Kristen. I don't have time except to say "Robert, drop her, she cheated on you & will again!"
October 23, 2012

"Michelle Malkin is a "dummy.""
October 25, 2012

"Now grotesque @BetteMidler is into the Trump act --- trying to become relevant again."
Oct. 28, 2012

"While @BetteMidler is an extremely unattractive woman, I refuse to say that because I always insist on being politically correct."
October 28, 2012

"Many people walked out of Madonna's concert when she told them to vote for Obama. Years ago I walked out because the concert was terrible."
October 29 2012

"Let's continue to destroy the competitiveness of our factories & manufacturing so we can fight mythical global warming. China is so happy!"
November 1, 2012

@MRbelzer is a stone cold loser with no talent--why did they ever put him on "Law and Order?"
November 6, 2012

"This election is a total sham and a travesty. We are not a democracy!"
Twitter, November 6, 2012

I love show "Law and Order" but the @MRbelzer casting is the worst ever. No talent—unwatchable!
November 6, 2012

"Pervert alert. @RepWeiner is back on twitter. All girls under the age of 18, block him immediately."
November 7, 2012

"Everybody wants me to talk about Robert Pattinson and not Brian Williams—I guess people just don't care about Brian!"
November 9, 2012

"Everybody"...again

"She's baaack! @Rosie needs me to salvage her dying career. But it won't help-- she's got no talent & no persona. Too many tv cancellations!"
November 9, 2012

"Thanks- many are saying I'm the best 140 character writer in the world. It's easy when it's fun".
November 10, 2012

"@cher--I don't wear a "rug"—it's mine. And I promise not to talk about your massive plastic surgeries that didn't work."
November 13, 2012

"@cher should spend more time focusing on her family and dying career!"
November 13, 2012

"After Friday's Twilight release, I hope Robert Pattinson will not be seen in public with Kristen--she will cheat on him again!"
November 13, 2012

"Graydon Carter? "Dummy.""
December 19, 2012

@DanForsley @VanityFair Wrong--Graydon Carter has no talent and looks like shit! Also, his food sucks!
December 20, 2012

In response to Carter's bad review of Trump Grill(e)

"@Deadspin guys are total losers—they had their story stolen right from under their bad complexions—other media capitalized!"
January 18, 2013

Deadspin responded with a simple "Fuck Off"...

@Deadspin's disgusting response will teach me & others not to be nice anymore—a sad lesson.
January 18, 2013

Nice! when did he start?

"Little @MacMiller, you illegally used my name for your song "Donald Trump" which now has over 75 million hits."
January 31, 2013

"Many people have commented that my fragrance, "Success" is the best scent & lasts the longest. Try it & let me know what you think!"
February 27, 2013

"Brian Williams is a "dummy.""
March 6, 2013

"Sorry folks, Donald Trump is much richer and far better looking than dopey @mcuban"
March 19, 2013

ROFL…He's an actual billionaire…as far as Donald's looks go…What if you took a 230lb inflamed pustule and dressed it up in Brooks Brothers?

"@michellemalkin Still waiting for coward @realDonaldTrump to tell me what in my "past" I should be ashamed of. #SmearMerchant"
Twitter, March 21, 2013

"@realDonaldTrump @michellemalkin You were born stupid!"
Twitter, March 22, 2013

"Rosie is crude, rude, obnoxious and dumb - other than that I like her very much!"
April 24, 2013

"I promise you that I'm much smarter than Jonathan Leibowitz -- I mean Jon Stewart @TheDailyShow. Who, by the way, is totally overrated."
April 24, 2013

"@richardroeper- Perhaps one of the worst replacements in showbiz, once you went on it was over! Your taste sucks!"
April 29, 2013

"Amazing how the haters & losers keep tweeting the name "F**kface Von Clownstick" like they are so original & like no one else is doing it…"
May 3, 2013

"Just tried watching Modern Family -- written by a moron, really boring. Writer has the mind of a very dumb and backward child. Sorry, Danny!"
June 13, 2013

"@Scribe53: @realDonaldTrump @MGIFINC Agree about Rosie. Sad because she is very talented." Actually, she has got no talent at all-ZERO!"
July 13, 2013

"Isn't it crazy that people of little or no talent or success can be so critical of those whose accomplishments are great with no retribution"
July 18, 2013

"Chuck Todd is a "moron.""
August 9, 2013

"You must admit that Bryant Gumbel is one of the dumbest racists around - an arrogant dope with no talent. Failed at CBS etc-why still on TV?"
August 20, 2013

"@realDonaldTrump Who does Bryant Gumbel think he's messing with?? He's such a condescending jerk!" And a no talent racist!"
August 20, 2013

"With the whacko pervert Weiner about to be embarrassed, all women need to be on the lookout. Sexting begins 9.11 @ 12:01 AM"
August 22, 2013

"Why are people upset w/ me over Pres Obama's birth certificate?I got him to release it, or whatever it was, when nobody else could!"
Twitter, August 22, 2013

"The people that gave you global warming are the same people that gave you ObamaCare!"
November 23, 2013

"We should be focused on magnificently clean and healthy air and not distracted by the expensive hoax that is global warming!"
December 6, 2013

"The con artists changed the name from GLOBAL WARMING to CLIMATE CHANGE when GLOBAL WARMING was no longer working and credibility was lost!"
December 30, 2013

"Any and all weather events are used by the GLOBAL WARMING HOAXSTERS to justify higher taxes to save our planet! They don't believe it $$$$!"
January 26, 2014

"When will our country stop wasting money on global warming and so many other truly "STUPID" things and begin to focus on lower taxes?"
February 5, 2014

"@Michael_KSC: @realDonaldTrump @thedropkicks Whether Global Warming or Climate change. The fact is We didn't cause it. We cannot change it.
February 18, 2014

"Ellen was so awkward and insecure last night. The pizza skit was terrible. She should dump Andy Lassner, a guy with no absolutely no talent! "
March 3, 2014

"@mcuban says he is a member of Dallas National but doesn't play golf. Who is a member of a golf club that doesn't play?? No talent! @TMZ"
April 8, 2014

"Saw @mcuban try to hit a ball in Lake Tahoe while I played in tournament- he's got no talent or strength!!!! @TMZ"

April 8, 2014

"Rosie O'Donnell just said she felt "shame" at being fat-not politically correct! She killed Star Jones for weight loss surgery, just had it!"

May 9 2014

"Many people have said I'm the world's greatest writer of 140 character sentences."

July 21, 2014

"That Seth Meyers is hosting the Emmy Awards is a total joke. He is very awkward with almost no talent. Marbles in his mouth!"

August 25, 2014

"I will be releasing the full interview with a guy named Baxter @antbaxter only to show the bias and stupidity of him and @BBCWorld. Clowns!"
      September 28, 2014

"Every time I speak of the haters and losers I do so with great love and affection. They cannot help the fact that they were born fucked up!"
      September 28, 2014

"Russell Brand is a "major loser!""
      October 16, 2014

"There are many Jonathan Gruber types selling the global warming "stuff" - and they really do believe the American public is stupid."
      November 18, 2014

"Dummy Bill Maher did an advertisement for the failing New York Times where the picture of him is very sad-he looks pathetic, bloated & gone!"
December 23, 2014

Worst graphics and stage backdrop ever at the Oscars. Show is terrible, really BORING!
February 22, 2015

"I wish everyone, including the haters and losers, a very happy Easter!"
April 5, 2015

"@laurasgoldman: .@realDonaldTrump why is it necessary to comment on .@ariannahuff looks?

"Because she is a dog who wrongfully comments on me"
April 6, 2015

"How much money is the extremely unattractive (both inside and out) Arianna Huffington paying her poor ex-hubby for the use of his name?"
April 6, 2015

"For all of the haters and losers out there sorry, I never went Bankrupt -- but I did build a world class company and employ many people!"
April 18, 2015

Four times....his companies went bankrupt four times

"National Review @NRO may be going out of business because of the really pathetic job being done by @JonahNRO. No talent means death - sad!"
April 20, 2015

"Nobody but Donald Trump will save Israel. You are wasting your time with these politicians and political clowns. Best!"
April 27, 2015

"Nobody would fight harder for free speech than me but why taunt, over and over again, in order to provoke possible death to audience. DUMB!"
May 4, 2015

"Deflategate: They had no definitive proof against Tom Brady or #patriots. If Hillary doesn't have to produce Emails, why should Tom? Very unfair!"
May 11, 2015

"I am the BEST builder, just look at what I've built. Hillary can't build. Republican candidates can't build. They don't have a clue!"
May 13, 2015

"All the haters & losers must admit that, unlike others, I never attacked dopey Jon Stewart for his phony last name. Would never do that!" — You have and you did, Mr. Drumpf.
June 1, 2015

"Jon Stewart is the most overrated joke on television. A wiseguy with no talent. Not smart, but convinces dopes he is! Fading out fast."
June 1, 2015

"Sleep eyes @ChuckTodd is killing Meet The Press. Isn't he pathetic? Love watching him fail!"
July 12, 2015

"The worst show in Las Vegas, in my opinion, is @pennjillette. Hokey garbage. New York show even worse!"
July 16, 2015

"Isn't it funny that I am now #1 in the money losing @HuffingtonPost (poll), and by a big margin. Dummy @ariannahuff must be thrilled!"
July 25, 2015

"How can a dummy dope like Harry Hurt, who wrote a failed book about me but doesn't know me or anything about me, be on TV discussing Trump?"
July 29, 2015

"Megyn Kelly is a "bimbo.""
Twitter, Aug. 7, 2015

Megan Kelly Rocks!

"@FrankLuntz is a low class slob who came to my office looking for consulting work and I had zero interest. Now he picks anti-Trump panels!"
August 7, 2015

"The president of the pathetic Club For Growth came to my office in N.Y.C. and asked for a ridiculous $1,000,000 contribution. I said no way!"
September 1, 2015

"Really dumb @CheriJacobus. Begged my people for a job. Turned her down twice and she went hostile. Major loser, zero credibility!"
> **February 5, 2016**

"There are no buyers for the worthless @NYDailyNews but little Mort Zuckerman is frantically looking. It is bleeding red ink - a total loser! "
> **February 11, 2016**

"Have a good chance to win Texas on Tuesday. Cruz is a nasty guy, not one Senate endorsement and, despite talk, gets nothing done. Loser!"
> **February 26, 2016**

"Phony Club For Growth tried to shake me down for one million dollars, & is now putting out nasty negative ads on me. They are total losers!"
> **March 9, 2016**

"If crazy @megynkelly didn't cover me so much on her terrible show, her ratings would totally tank. She is so average in so many ways!"
March 19, 2016

"I will be the best by far in fighting terror. I'm the only one that was right from the beginning, & now Lyin' Ted & others are copying me."
March 23, 2016

"@CNN is so negative, getting even worse as I get closer. Just had two anti-Trump losers with zero rebuttal from my team. Turning off!"
May 21, 2016

"Mitt Romney had his chance to beat a failed president but he choked like a dog. Now he calls me racist-but I am least racist person there is"
June 11, 2016

"Justice Ginsburg of the U.S. Supreme Court has embarrassed all by making very dumb political statements about me. Her mind is shot - resign!"
July 12, 2016

"Tried watching low-rated @Morning_Joe this morning, unwatchable! @morningmika is off-the-wall, a neurotic and not very bright mess!"
Twitter, August 22, 2016

Mika called out Trump's stump speeches as sounding like he drinks a lot.

"Some day, when things calm down, I'll tell the real story of @JoeNBC and his very insecure long-time girlfriend @morningmika. Two clowns!"
August 22, 2016

"It is being reported by virtually everyone, and is a fact, that the media pile on against me is the worst in American political history!"
August 23, 2016

"@CNN just doesn't get it, and that's why their ratings are so low - and getting worse. Boring anti-Trump panelists, mostly losers in life!"
September 17, 2016

"Wow Crooked Hillary was duped and used by my worst Miss U. Hillary Floated her and an "angel" without checking her past, which is terrible!"
September 30, 2016

"Anytime you see a story about me or my campaign saying "sources said," DO NOT believe it. There are no sources, they are just made up lies!"
September 30, 2016

"Using Alicia M in the debate as a paragon of virtue just shows that Crooked Hillary suffers from BAD JUDGEMENT! Hillary was set up by a con."
September 30, 2016

"Did Crooked Hillary help disgusting (check out sex tape and past) Alicia M become a U.S. citizen so she could use her in the debate?"
September 30, 2016

"The ONLY bad thing about winning the Presidency is that I did not have the time to go through a long but winning trial on Trump U. Too bad!"
November 19, 2016

"I watched parts of @nbcsnl Saturday Night Live last night. It is a totally one-sided, biased show - nothing funny at all. Equal time for us?"
November 20, 2016

Who is "us?" This is how it works now. You got elected and for four years people are going to criticize and satirize you…T'was ever thus.

"In addition to winning the Electoral College in a landslide, I won the popular vote if you deduct the millions of people who voted illegally"
November 27, 2016

"@HighonHillcrest: @jeffzeleny what PROOF do u have DonaldTrump did not suffer from millions of FRAUD votes? Journalist? Do your job! @CNN"
November 28, 2016

"@Filibuster: @jeffzeleny Pathetic - you have no sufficient evidence that Donald Trump did not suffer from voter fraud, shame! Bad reporter.
November 28, 2016

"Nobody should be allowed to burn the American flag - if they do, there must be consequences - perhaps loss of citizenship or year in jail!"
November 29, 2016

"Just tried watching Saturday Night Live - unwatchable! Totally biased, not funny and the Baldwin impersonation just can't get any worse. Sad"
December 4, 2016

Now, for your amusement, here is a Twitter feud between a writer from Modern Family and Donald Trump:

 Donald J. Trump @realDonaldTrump   12 Jun
I've been warning about China since as early as the 80's. No one wanted to listen. Now our country is in real trouble. #TimetoGetTough
Retweeted by Danny Zuker
Collapse ← Reply ↨ Retweet ★ Favorite ••• More

389 RETWEETS **123** FAVORITES

8:47 AM - 12 Jun 13 · Details

 Danny Zuker @DannyZuker   12 Jun
.@realDonaldTrump You've always been tough on China, sir. Particularly the children who make your shitty clothes. pic.twitter.com/6dp2omL1hZ
Hide photo ← Reply ↨ Retweet ★ Favorite ••• More

Donald J. Trump @realDonaldTrump 22h
.@DannyZuker Danny--You're a total loser!
Retweeted by Danny Zuker
Collapse ← Reply ⇅ Retweet ★ Favorite ••• More

99 RETWEETS **129** FAVORITES

12:26 PM - 12 Jun 13 · Details

 Danny Zuker @DannyZuker 22h
.@realDonaldTrump Your insults need work. Here's one I've been working on: "Every picture you post of yourself is a dick pic." See?
Collapse ← Reply ⇅ Retweet ★ Favorite ••• More

164 RETWEETS **400** FAVORITES

12:28 PM - 12 Jun 13 · Details

 Donald J. Trump @realDonaldTrump 21h
I can't resist hitting lightweight @DannyZuker verbally when he starts up because he is just.so pathetic and easy (stupid)!
Retweeted by Danny Zuker
Collapse ← Reply ⇅ Retweet ★ Favorite ••• More

37 RETWEETS **24** FAVORITES

 Danny Zuker @DannyZuker 21h
.@realDonaldTrump Since you're unable to manufacture decent comebacks maybe you could outsource the job to China. #LOL #Trumpelstiltskin
Collapse ← Reply ⇅ Retweet ★ Favorite ••• More

197 RETWEETS **468** FAVORITES

Donald J. Trump @realDonaldTrump 16h
Lightweight @DannyZuker is too stupid to see that China (and others) is destroying the U.S. economically and our leaders are helpless! SAD.
Retweeted by Danny Zuker
Collapse ← Reply ↻ Retweet ★ Favorite ••• More

67 RETWEETS **39** FAVORITES

 Danny Zuker @DannyZuker 16h
.@realDonaldTrump I'm def too stupid to see how manufacturing your shitty clothes in China while you bloviate about them isn't hypocritical.
Collapse ← Reply ↻ Retweet ★ Favorite ••• More

146 RETWEETS **328** FAVORITES

 **Donald J. Trump** ✓
@realDonaldTrump

Just tried watching Modern Family - written by a moron, really boring. Writer has the mind of a very dumb and backward child. Sorry Danny!

← Reply ↻ Retweet ★ Favorite ••• More

140 RETWEETS **98** FAVORITES

Danny Zuker @DannyZuker 15h
.@realDonaldTrump Doesn't like the show I work on but then we've never tested well with the racist, hypocritical, multiple bankruptcy demo.
Collapse ← Reply ↕ Retweet ★ Favorite ••• More

215 RETWEETS   **452** FAVORITES

 Donald J. Trump @realDonaldTrump 15h
"@Leigh26Heather: @realDonaldTrump WHO ON EARTH IS DANNY ZUKER????!!!!" A lightweight moron who only gets attention by attacking Trump.
↻ Retweeted by Danny Zuker
Collapse ← Reply ↕ Retweet ★ Favorite ••• More

32 RETWEETS   **26** FAVORITES

 Danny Zuker @DannyZuker 15h
Clearly the one thing @realDonaldTrump DIDN'T inherit from his daddy was a thesaurus. #Loser #Dummy #Lightweight
Collapse ← Reply ↕ Retweet ★ Favorite ••• More

69 RETWEETS   **196** FAVORITES

7:06 PM - 12 Jun 13 · Details

 Danny Zuker @DannyZuker 15h
Bye for now, @realDonaldTrump. I have a busy night of not grandstanding to put the wrong people to death in the Central Park Mugging case.
Collapse ← Reply ↕ Retweet ★ Favorite ••• More

34 RETWEETS   **112** FAVORITES

7:11 PM - 12 Jun 13 · Details

Also by Jules Carlysle

DUMBASS

Joss Whedon: The Making of a Cult Superhero (with Hubert O'Hearn)

The Doggy Business Book for Kids

Made in the USA
Charleston, SC
28 December 2016